ASPHALT GODS

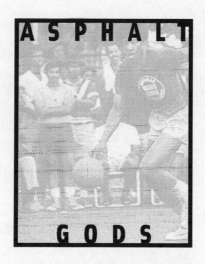

ASPHALT GODS

An Oral History of the Rucker Tournament

Vincent M. Mallozzi

DOUBLEDAY

NEW YORK   LONDON   TORONTO   SYDNEY   AUCKLAND

PUBLISHED BY DOUBLEDAY
a division of Random House, Inc.

A hardcover edition of this book was published in 2003 by Doubleday.

www.doubleday.com

Book design by Chris Welch
Original jacket design by Jesse Reyes

The Library of Congress has cataloged the hardcover edition as:

Library of Congress Cataloging-in-Publication Data
Mallozzi, Vincent M.
Asphalt gods : an oral history of the Rucker Tournament /
Vincent M. Mallozzi.
p. cm.
1. Rucker Tournament (Basketball)—History. 2. Basketball—
Tournaments—New York (State)—Harlem (New York)—History.
I. Title.
GV885.49.R83M35 2003
796.323'6—dc21
2003043538

First trade paperback edition published 2006
Hardcover Edition ISBN: 0-385-50675-9
Trade Paperback ISBN 13: 978-0-385-52099-7
Trade Paperback ISBN: 0-385-52099-9

145038997

To Christopher—My Heart

And Michael—My Soul

ACKNOWLEDGMENTS

I would like to thank the following:

Ernie Morris, without whom this book could not have been written. Ernie, a Holcombe Rucker disciple who once played in the tournament, not only shared his great memories but helped me gain access to past Rucker stars who were gracious enough to pass along their own stories.

I would also like to thank Mary Rucker Thomas, Lou Carnesecca, Peter Vecsey, Rodney Williams, Julius Erving, Cal Ramsey, John Isaacs, Howie Evans, Joe Hammond, Pee Wee Kirkland, Greg Marius, Mel Feldman, Aaron Donovan, Grant Glickson, Anthony Artuso, Elena Gustines, Noam Cohen, Alex Evans, Joe Brescia, Julius Greene, John Alessi, Tony Callano, Joe Colitto, and Fred Bierman.

And to my wife, Cathy, who understood how important it was for me to write this book. I love you.

CONTENTS

INTRODUCTION

alf-Man, Half-Amazing took a pass in the low post and spun to his right, where Captain Nappy and two other defenders from Murder Inc. were waiting with outstretched arms. Surrounded but not surrendering, the powerful forward soared north toward the rim. He rose above the pack with a basketball held high in his left hand, and sent through the cords a vicious dunk that shook the Harlem faithful out of their seats in the summer of 2002. At courtside, the play-by-play man shouted, "Ohhhh, ladies and gentlemen, that move was half man, and yes—it was half amazing!"

Scenes like these, involving players with nicknames as colorful and creative as their games, can be viewed only at Holcombe Rucker Park on 155th Street and Eighth Avenue, across the street from the site of the old Polo Grounds, where project buildings now cover the same earth that Willie Mays once did for the New York Giants.

Every summer, thousands of fans flock to see local heroes like Half-Man, Half-Amazing and Captain Nappy do basketball battle beneath the bright lights on a stage built by the man for whom the world's most famous outdoor arena is named; a stage that for more than half a century has been bringing together the best amateur and professional basketball players from around the globe.

In the place where local legends like Jackie Jackson, Joe Hammond, and Pee Wee Kirkland came to chase a dream, and world-class superstars like Wilt Chamberlain and Julius Erving came to share one, the cheers and chants still tumble from the rooftops and tree limbs, and from high atop the chain-link fence that surrounds the mythical park.

"It was," Hall of Famer Julius Erving said to me years after his legendary battles at Rucker Park, "a bone-chilling experience."

For the past seventeen years I have been fortunate enough to sit in the stone bleachers that overlook the hallowed, wind-swept patch of blacktop where these asphalt gods have been soaring into basketball folklore for generations. Their stories, most of which have never been recorded, form the backbone of this book. As a kid who grew up in Harlem playing and watching the game, and following the moves of these gifted players on and off the court, *Asphalt Gods* is a book I was born to write.

Since 1986, I've been covering the action at Rucker Park for publications like the *New York Times*, *Village Voice*, *Slam*, *Source*, and *Vibe* magazines. My *Vibe* feature story on the Rucker Tournament a few summers back caught the attention of an editor at Doubleday, which led to the idea for this book.

My in-depth coverage of playground basketball has taken me deeper into this world than any other scribe has ever journeyed. In fact, very little has ever been written about the brilliant games on the blacktop and the magical moves created by players who are mostly unknown beyond the chain-link fences that surround their legend. In recognition of the many tales from the blacktop I've conveyed to readers throughout the years, I was recently inducted into the media wing of the Pro Rucker Hall of Fame, an honor I deeply cherish.

In the absence of formal playground records, I felt compelled to write this book, and share with basketball audiences everywhere snippets of real-life hoop theater that most roundball fans were not fortunate enough to have enjoyed.

Since the early 1950s the Rucker Tournament has served as a blueprint for outdoor hoop leagues across the nation. The world-renowned Baker League in Philadelphia, the second-oldest outdoor league in the nation, was created in the image of West Harlem's summertime showcase. The Rucker League featured a brand of stylish and innovative basketball that began adding a colorful flavor to the stiff and slower-paced version of the game being played at the collegiate and professional levels, ultimately changing it forever.

"There would not be an NBA as we know it," Pee Wee Kirkland said, "if it were not for Holcombe Rucker."

At its height in the early 1970s, when players like Erving, the great Dr. J., were doing battle with playground phenoms like Joe Hammond, Rucker Park was an unofficial summer training camp for NBA players and others who dreamed of wearing a pro uniform.

Indeed, a number of Rucker players throughout the years have used the exposure and experience they gained in the mythical park to help pave a road toward professional basketball careers. Current NBA players Mark Jackson, Ron Artest, and Stephon Marbury are all Rucker Park alums.

"The reputation of Rucker Park is known throughout the world," said Artest, a New Yorker who has emerged as a star with the Indiana Pacers. "If you can turn heads playing in the Rucker Tournament, you can turn heads anywhere."

The basketball playground where I spent the summers of my youth, where I received an early education in roundball, was not

Rucker Park but another playground in Harlem that cut right through the heart of my two worlds.

I lived at 512 East 119th Street, on the south side of the park adjacent to Public School 206, in a tired brownstone not unlike the others lived in mostly by Italian folk—family and friends among them—whose ancestors had settled there at the tail end of the nineteenth century.

On the park's north side stood the Wagner Projects, low-income housing units of mostly black families where one could find some of the world's greatest basketball players, none greater than Hammond, the playground prodigy whose legend was intact long before I picked up a basketball.

For twenty years I played basketball in that park with my Italian friends, those kids mostly from blue-collar families, from a land of mobsters and cappuccino and Sinatra soundtracks that made Pleasant Avenue the wiseguy capital of the world.

And I played with and against the black kids from Wagner and nearby neighborhoods, awesome players who always brought their A-game to the park, making all of us much better players in the end.

Every sweaty day, from the moment the sun rose out of the East River until long after it had disappeared behind the old tenement buildings on Harlem's west side, both cultures collided on the asphalt. The white kids always pretended to be the Boston Celtics, trying to imitate Larry Bird or Kevin McHale or Danny Ainge. The black kids did their best to imitate Boston's hated rivals, the predominantly black Los Angeles Lakers of Magic Johnson, Kareem Abdul-Jabbar, and James Worthy.

When I wasn't playing ball, I was watching it in places like the Wagner Center on East 120th Street, the place where the great Earl Monroe once ran his summer academy. In 1978, I was the sixth man on a team called the Bucketheads that finished out of the playoffs, the lone white face on a gymnasium floor shared by five hundred black players who were a part of Earl The Pearl's summer camp. There, The Pearl taught us the fine art of boxing out, and gifted NBA point guards like Calvin Murphy and Tiny Archibald taught us how to dribble.

I also saw classic hoop battles at the La Guardia Memorial House on East 116th Street and at the outdoor courts in Jefferson Park on 114th Street.

But nowhere else could I find the kind of basketball that was being played at Rucker Park, where legends, nicknames, and great rivalries are born every summer, where reputations can die on a single play, and where magic still fills the air on hot summer nights in Harlem.

By the time I left the old neighborhood in 1989, the sounds of Sinatra had faded into summer winds past. The Pleasant Avenue that I knew was nearly gone, but the basketball memories that helped shape my life—from playing the game at St. Agnes High School to covering it as sports editor of the *St. John's Today* when Lou Carnesecca's Redmen were reaching the Final Four in 1985—the game that influenced my decision to become a sportswriter, was still very much a part of me.

And all the great players I've met along the way, especially those who take their duffel bags and fancy games to Rucker Park, have become a lot more to me than mere human interest stories. They are neighbors and friends, guys I grew up with in and around the old neighborhood.

Seeing them on that fabled court, talking to them, and sharing their incredible stories with basketball fans who have seen too little of these playground warriors has become my favorite pastime.

Chapter 1

THE PIED PIPER

O n March 2, 1926, Holcombe Rucker came into a hard life. He was raised in poverty by his grandmother, Rosa Deniston, who struggled to make the rent at 141st Street and Bradhurst Avenue. He was a star guard at Benjamin Franklin High School in East Harlem, but dropped out to go off to serve in the United States Army during World War II. By the time Uncle Sam sent him home in 1946, he was a mature and extremely focused young man.

That year, Rucker came back to Harlem and earned a general equivalency high school diploma, then enrolled at CCNY,

Holcombe Rucker in a suit (*New York Times*)

where he took night classes and needed just three years to complete a four-year bachelor of arts degree. He landed a job as a recreational director with the New York City Department of Parks; taught English at Harlem's Junior High School 139, and worked at St. Phillips, a local parish church and community center at 134th Street between Seventh and Eighth Avenues, where he served as a basketball coach and created a basketball tournament that featured divisions made up of various age groups. The purpose of the tournament was to keep neighborhood kids off the streets and out of trouble. Through lessons learned in the discipline and dedication it took to become a winning basketball team, Rucker was able to teach his players a lot about life. Most of these players were living in poverty as well, and Rucker wanted them to make something of themselves so that they could avoid the kind of hard life he had known as a child.

Charles Turner, a Rucker disciple, played for Holcombe Rucker at St. Phillips. "I played for the Mites," Turner said, "before I graduated to the Midgets."

Turner is sixty-five now, but he "can remember like yesterday" the day his life was turned around by Rucker at halftime of a weekend game between St. Phillips and a powerhouse team from Harlem's YMCA.

At the time, Turner was a fourteen-year-old hotshot from Central Needle Trade High School with a lot of attitude but not much discipline.

"We went out on the court that day and just started clowning around, trying to make fancy passes and just do our own thing," Turner said. "We were just kids, I guess, just having fun."

At halftime, St. Phillips trailed the YMCA by 30 points.

Holcombe Rucker, not smiling on this day, sat his team down
in the locker room. He hesitated a moment before he spoke, his
gentle eyes sweeping over every one of them. And then he let
loose.

"I put all of this training into every one of you, all of this
time!" Rucker shrieked. "And you're out there bullshitting?"

Rucker paused again, burning a look into his players. As he
stared long and hard, tears began to stream down his cheeks.

"We were frozen scared," Turner said. "We were all tough kids
from the streets. We had never seen a grown man cry before."

Rucker never said another word.

"He didn't have to," Turner said. "It was a lesson in discipline
and respect that we would never forget."

Turner and his teammates went out and completely dominated the second half, grabbing every rebound, hustling for
every loose ball.

"Those kids from the Y were looking at us like we were pos-
sessed or something," Turner said. "We ended up winning that
game by 30 points."

Charles Turner still lives in Harlem, and so too does the memory of Holcombe Rucker, who left New York City a basketball
treasure that still bears his name. The legacy of Turner's mentor
is everywhere. It lives in Harlem classrooms and barrooms, in
gymnasiums and living rooms, and it was alive and well one frigid
day at Charles Restaurant in Harlem, just a bounce pass from
Rucker Park, where Turner and Ernie Morris, a Rucker historian, were wearing sour faces over their sweet yams.

"Earl Manigault needed to be smacked, literally smacked to
degrade Rucker like that," said the fifty-nine-year-old Morris,
spearing his ham hocks as he spoke. "I mean, Rucker wasn't a fat

guy who earned a living cleaning parks, the man was a Parks Department director who helped thousands of us Harlem kids go to
college, and kept thousands more off the streets and out of jail."

On a winter's day in the basketball capital of the universe, a
hot lunch is spoiled when Turner brings up the movie *Rebound:
The Legend of Earl "The Goat" Manigault*, which was broadcast
with a great deal of fanfare on HBO.

Don Cheadle plays the Goat, a high-flying dunking machine
with a heroin problem who gets swallowed up by the same mean
streets he once soared over (we'll hear a great deal about him
in the chapters to follow). Forest Whitaker plays Holcombe
Rucker, who speaks words of wisdom while standing behind a
garbage pail, a broom, and a big belly.

"Earl was a consultant on the set," says Turner. "I liked the
Goat a whole lot, but why did he have to describe Mr. Rucker
like that to those movie people? It just didn't make any sense."

Perhaps no one knew Holcombe Rucker, the man, better
than Morris and Turner, both high school hoop stars from the
1950s who learned their games under him at St. Phillips. According to them, Rucker was all about one thing, helping kids,
especially troubled kids. He was not, they insist, "some fool
Parks Department custodian" they had read about throughout
the years in newspapers and magazines or seen portrayed on
television.

"When you played ball for him, you learned to answer every
one of his questions with a 'yes sir,' or a 'no sir,' " Turner said.
"And don't even think about playing ball unless Mr. Rucker took
a look at your report card and approved of it."

In the summer of 1946, Rucker began staging an outdoor
tournament on 138th Street between Lenox and Fifth Avenues.

Those early outdoor tourneys opened with four teams and one referee, Rucker himself.

In time, Rucker's vision expanded, and he began scheduling games for his playground teams against other youth organizations throughout New York City. Those who knew Rucker well say he managed his youth leagues despite a lack of cooperation from the Department of Parks, which turned its back on him. There were times, friends say, when Rucker would have to scrape up loose change to buy a whistle, and others when he had to borrow basketballs from some of the kids playing in his games.

The late John "Twenty Grand" Hunter, a dapper "street entrepreneur with his ear to the street" as one player from those days describes him, often slipped Rucker a few dollars when the going got real tight. Though Hunter earned much of his money through sports gambling on events like horse racing and football games, he was always generous with his profits where Holcombe Rucker was concerned. If Rucker's kids needed uniforms or sneakers and couldn't afford them, Hunter went deep into his pockets. Hunter also provided transportation money for players traveling to and from games, and he made sure that every car or bus that transported the players had a full tank of gas.

Ernie Morris remembers playing on those early Rucker teams, and competing against the very best that the city had to offer: "Hook or crook, Holcombe had us on the move," he said. "We played against black kids from the Bronx, Irish and Italian kids from Hell's Kitchen, anyone who wanted to give us a game."

A Date with Mary

Holcombe Rucker's hoop dream was slowly coming into focus on an April night in 1947, when a friend asked if he would do him a favor and take his date, a young woman named Mary Green, to a Billie Holiday performance at Small's Paradise Club on 135th Street and Seventh Avenue. Rucker's friend had made other plans that evening, and though he and Mary were not seriously involved, he did not want to hurt her feelings.

"But I have my own date tonight," Holcombe told his friend.

"Please," Holcombe's friend replied. "Just do me this favor, just this once."

So Holcombe took Mary to Small's, which ranked in Harlem and show business legends with the old Cotton Club and the Savoy Ballroom. It was the place where Harlem's elite gathered for good times when talents like Holiday, Bessie Smith, Ethel Waters, Billy Eckstine, Lena Horne, Duke Ellington, Count Basie, and Bill Robinson dominated the stage.

"Holcombe had a date and told her to meet him there," Mary Rucker Thomas recently recalled. "But when his girlfriend came in, I guess she saw us together, and she just went and sat somewhere else."

And Mary's original date?

"He just never showed up, and Holcombe knew he wasn't going to," she recalled. "So Holcombe just stayed there with me and we listened to Billie Holiday together. I thought to myself, 'Here's a real nice guy.' "

Eight months later, Mary and Holcombe were married.

"It was a December wedding," she said, "a beautiful December wedding."

By 1949, two years after Holcombe and Mary wed, Rucker's tournament had moved to the St. Nicholas Houses playground on 128th Street and Seventh Avenue. The park there soon became Rucker's office, a weathered green bench serving as his office chair, an old streetlamp his night-light. There, scores of young black men and women, many from single-parent households, some of whom did not even play basketball, showed up daily for some good, old-fashioned Holcombe advice, finding stability and comfort, guidance and assurance, and ultimately proper direction in their mentor's words.

Harlem's Pied Piper, Rucker spent fourteen and fifteen hours a day in that park. He ate dinner there, his favorite meal a Chinese dish of vegetables and rice with heavy brown gravy. Dessert always came in two courses: a cup of coffee followed by a cigarette. He'd arrive most mornings by 8:30, often finding some kids already waiting for him. For many of them, Rucker's park was a home away from home. "Each one, teach one," was his motto; it would later become the name of a Harlem youth organization run by his disciples.

The Pied Piper imparted his wisdom to talented but underprivileged Harlem hoopsters, hundreds of whom he helped steer off the streets and toward college and a better life. These were kids who perfected their moves on playground courts throughout the city, bringing to the blacktop the grit, muscle, and determination it took to survive on the mean streets where they were raised. That brand of hard-nosed basketball, combined with high-flying, artistic moves to the basket created during years of one-on-one and full-scale battles on the asphalt, became in essence the true identity of the city game, separating it from the way the game was being played in places like Indiana, the result of a car accident that nearly took his life on April 23, 1984.

"I was young and foolish at the time," he said, "and when I came home, I found that people were more or less ashamed about what had taken place."

A fallen idol whose ticket to fame was torn by greed and youthful naïveté, Warner had few places to turn when he left Rikers for home. Of the thousands of Harlem kids who once looked up to him, few were willing to even give the disgraced star a game of one-on-one.

Ed Warner was now a complete outcast in a world he once conquered. That's when Holcombe Rucker found him.

"Holcombe came to me and said, 'Hey, Ed, I'm not condoning what you fellows did, but I believe that to err is human, to forgive divine.'

"He said, 'I'm gonna give you fellows an opportunity to redeem yourselves.' He was referring to the guys involved in the scandal. I still get goose bumps when I remember him telling me, 'You fellows were young and you didn't know what you were doing. But I'm going to give you an opportunity to come back to your community and let the people know that you made a mistake as a youngster and you tried very hard to correct the mistakes that you made. I'm forming this tournament, and I'd like very much for you to be a part of it.'

"I was so moved, so touched by that act of kindness," Warner said. "I said that I would definitely play in his tournament. He opened the door for us."

Warner, Layne, and Roman soon began playing in the college division of the Rucker Tournament, winning over fans with the kind of stellar play that made City College a basketball treasure.

During the NBA season, the trio spent their weekends driving together to play basketball in the Eastern League.

"The scandal formed our bond," said Warner, who earned extra money working as a high school referee. He was an observer of officials for New York City's Public Schools Athletic League (PSAL) as well as a recreational supervisor in Harlem up until his death.

"We weren't seasoned criminals, and we didn't receive the guidance we should have," he said. "It's too bad a man like Holcombe Rucker hadn't entered our lives a lot sooner than he did."

Chapter 2

THE PROS COME TO HARLEM

By 1953, Rucker's tourney had expanded to a two-tiered league that featured both a high school and college division. The games were held that year at St. Nicholas playground on 128th Street and Seventh Avenue.

The following year, Rucker put together his final dream, a pro division of his tournament that would fast make "The Rucker" a household name throughout New York City and beyond. It would bring together pro talent from all over the country and set up the pro versus playground mystique that would become Rucker Park's signature for the next five decades.

At the time there were no official NBA summer leagues, training camps, or workout facilities for players to stay in shape and keep a sharp competitive edge in their off-season. But there was Rucker Park, and when word spread about the caliber of talent that Holcombe Rucker had assembled in his park, it wasn't long before pro players began wanting a piece of the action.

With Rucker's league growing in size and stature, it was moved in 1954 to a large park on 130th Street and Seventh Avenue. Top teams from New Jersey, Philadelphia, and Washington, D.C., began to arrive to do hoop war with some of New York's finest players. Still, the Department of Parks continued to give short shrift to its own employee, denying Rucker's request to erect portable bleachers to keep fans comfortable. Meanwhile, portable bleachers along large stretches of fashionable Fifth Avenue were rotting in the sun.

Nevertheless, on warm summer weekends, thousands of Harlemites and hoop junkies from around the city began showing up for the best brand of basketball money couldn't buy. So did legions of coaches, talent scouts, and other recruiters who often "discovered" players in the park.

The scene was carnival-like, with pushcart vendors hawking beer and ice cream, old ladies selling fried chicken at 25 cents a piece, and fans in the corners of the park huddled over small flames cooking up mickeys (sweet potatoes) in pans from their own kitchens. Little children stood on milk crates to get a better look at the action while their parents worked out their vocal cords along the sidelines, watching skilled men in tank tops and shorts take a boy's game to the level of a new, freestyle form of art. People riding past the park on green city buses often jockeyed for window space to catch a glimpse of the action.

"I can't think of a great player who didn't play up there in those days," said Lou Carnesecca, the legendary St. John's coach who is now retired. Carnesecca, a high school coach in those days, made a number of trips to Rucker Park, often scouting players in the high school division. The coach often stopped in on the professional action, wanting to see for himself what everyone else in the city was talking about.

"The games, the players, the crowds, oh man, you had to see it to believe it," said Carnesecca. "And the best part is that all the people at those great games saw all that unbelievable talent for free."

Indeed, this wasn't the kind of stiff, stuffy, structured hoops found at the college or professional levels and taught by mostly white, starch-collared coaches with crew cuts. It was instead a mostly black, free-flowing, loosey-goosey, wide-open, one-on-one, run-and-gun, behind-your-back, between-your-legs, shake-and-bake, in-your-face makeover of James Naismith's original game. X's and O's were now being replaced by "ooohhhs" and "ahhhs." Those free-spirited moves that came not from a playbook but from the pages of the players' own imaginations would eventually weave their way into the fabric of the slower-paced professional game, changing it forever.

Ed Warner's Big Five

Pros who flocked to the park in those early days included players like Isaac "Rabbit" Walthour, one of the first true playground stars from New York. Walthour, a cerebral and lightning-quick six two point guard who played briefly with the Milwaukee Bucks in the 1953–54 season, was well known in basketball circles as being one of the first black players to try out for an NBA team.

"Rabbit was a basketball genius who came before Joe Hammond and Pee Wee Kirkland and all them guys," Carl Green said. "He could shoot and pass. He knew the game. He could set people up like Jason Kidd does nowadays. He was so damn fast, man."

Walthour played on a talented Rucker bomb squad called Ed Warner's Big Five, a run-and-gun team whose biggest star was Warner himself. Putting the team together was Warner's way of thanking the Pied Piper for giving him back a few rays of sunshine.

"Where I grew up downtown, the black guys tried to play a big man's game, similar to what white guys were playing back then," Green said. "By that I mean they tried to slow the ball down, move it over here and over there before shooting, they were black coaches just following suit.

"But uptown, at the Harlem Boys Club where Ed Warner grew up, they didn't play that way. They played fast break and would run you out of the gym. Ed Warner didn't play a slow, big man's game, he was quick, and he was better than a lot of guys already playing in the NBA."

One of Warner's psychological tricks in those Rucker days was the uniform he'd wear, or wouldn't wear, to tournament games. "Big Ed," as he was sometimes called, often suited up in a T-shirt and his Sunday dress pants—"the guys used to call them my funeral pants," he said—to play at the park. According to Green and others who were there, Big Ed always wore one pant leg cuffed up just below the knee and a different sneaker on each foot. A colored handkerchief surrounded his "permed, wavy hairdo," which left many opposing players thinking Big Ed was there simply to mess with them.

The rest of Ed Warner's Big Five included two streetball wizards named Herman Taylor and Cliff Williams at guard. The front line featured the low-post greatness of Warner, who teamed with a pair of slick-shooting centers named Shot Hayes and George Archer, and a six three shot-blocking demon named Donald "Cat" Hines, a north-and-south leaper whom Warner referred to as "the Dennis Rodman from back in the day."

The coach of Ed Warner's Big Five, John Isaacs, was already a Harlem legend long before he strolled along the sidelines at the Rucker Tournament. Isaacs had built his reputation as a superstar player for the mythical Harlem Renaissance, an all-black

professional team that barnstormed around the country during
the Depression years. At one point the Rens built a phenomenal
eighty-eight-game winning streak, which was snapped in 1933
by the rival Original Celtics, an all-white, New York City–based
team led by Nat Holman, who would later coach that great City
College squad to their double crown, and Joe Lapchick, who as
a coach would win four NIT titles at St. John's from the 1940s
through the 1960s. (The two teams would meet seven more
times, and the Rens would win each time.)

**A legendary performer for the Harlem Rens, John Isaacs was
one of the first coaches at Rucker Park.** (*John Isaacs*)

In Isaac's younger days the Rens used the Renaissance Casino
Ballroom in Harlem as their home court, sharing the same floor
with the big bands of Count Basie and Jimmy Lunceford.

IMOND — "The Destroyer", a
ayground leagues. Joe became d
ards when he joined Raskin's A
e age of 19. He averaged 19.
rookie season. Drafted by t

Joe Hammond, Allentown Jets Yearbook, circa 1970 *(Allentown Jets)*

Nicknamed "Wonder Boy" by team owner Bob Douglas, Isaacs was a key member of the 1939–40 Harlem Rens squad that captured the first world professional championship. In the final of that tournament, held in Chicago, the Rens, who stockpiled black superstars like William "Pop" Gates—a member of basketball's Hall of Fame—Wee Willie Smith, and Charles "Tarzan" Cooper, defeated the Oshkosh All-Stars of the fledgling National Basketball League.

Isaacs, six two, later joined another all-black professional squad, the Washington Bears, which he led to the world professional championship in 1943, scoring a game-high 11 points in the final to help defeat Oshkosh 43–31.

John Wooden, architect of the great UCLA Bruins teams that included Kareem Abdul-Jabbar and later Bill Walton, called those Rens "the greatest team I ever saw."

To no one's shock, Ed Warner's Big Five reached the finals of Rucker's initial pro tournament. But to the surprise of many, a bunch of talented upstarts on a team called Snooky's Sugar Bowl, named after a luncheonette on 137th Street and Seventh Avenue, also reached the finals.

Snooky's, led by a playground coach named John Walker, featured Warner's nineteen-year-old protégé Green, and Jack Defares, a sweet-shooting swingman who played his high school ball at Commerce. Green and Defares, widely considered among the best players ever to come out of the Big Apple, are both members of the New York City Hall of Fame. Snooky's also featured players like Buddy Thompson, a six four forward who just missed catching on with the Baltimore Bullets in 1954, and schoolyard veterans Timmy Vincent, a six four forward, and Buster Johnson, a six one guard.

"Me and my little crew used to go around from park to park playing for money," said Green, a schoolboy star at Benjamin Franklin High School in Harlem. "We played anybody for money, so when Rucker first approached me to play in his tournament, I was like, 'Nah man, I don't want to play in no tournament if money ain't involved.' But then he told me about Ed and all them other guys who were going to play in it, and I said, 'I'm in, Holcombe.' "

That first championship game brought thousands of people to the park, many of whom simply double- and triple-parked on busy Seventh Avenue. Police, lacking the manpower to tow all the cars, simply closed the avenue to traffic, then tried to get seats themselves to the highly anticipated showdown.

From the opening tip, players from both sides remember the game being nip and tuck, with the lead changing hands several times in the first half on the big chalk scoreboard that Rucker often monitored himself. Rabbit Walthour wowed the crowd by repeatedly breaking down the Snooky's defense. The Rabbit would storm toward the tin, wait for defenders to collapse on him, and then skip the rock to Warner or Archer, who always knew what to do with it.

Late in the second half, Warner began to wreak havoc beneath the offensive glass, taking the Rabbit's passes and rising high over outstretched fingertips to bury short jumpers, or using an assortment of head fakes to get defenders airborne and then slipping past them for a layup. The court at the time had an extended baseline area behind the basket, and Warner often took advantage of the extra space by driving past the defense and wrapping his body around the foul pole for a reverse layup.

Warner's magical moves that day earned him another nickname, "Genie," but more important, he was becoming a hero again in his hometown.

Somewhere, the Pied Piper was smiling.

Though no one can recall particular scores at any point in the game, Green remembers Snooky's being down by two points with less than two minutes to play in the contest.

"I remember dribbling the ball out on the wing and Shot Hayes trying to intimidate me," Green said. "He was saying things like, 'C'mon kid, bring it to me,' and 'Where you going? Give the ball up.' "

As Hayes yapped, Green kept his dribble up and looked away, as if he were thinking pass. Then suddenly, Green left Hayes's mouth open, and the mouths of the thousands watching, by slipping the ball through Hayes's legs, darting past him, catching it on the first bounce, and laying the ball softly through the cords to tie the game.

On the sidelines, Isaacs fumed.

"I heard Isaacs yell to Hayes, 'The next time he comes in that way, knock him on his ass.' "

In the closing seconds, though, the Genie worked his magic again and Ed Warner's Big Five pulled away to win the contest by three points.

"We won that game, and we were thrilled," said Isaacs, eighty-seven, who still coaches basketball at the Madison Square Boys Club in the Bronx.

"But, you know," he said, "I thought about that game as the years went on, and I got to thinking that it was actually kind of sad because Ed Warner should have been making all of those great moves in the pros, and not just at the Rucker."

Ed Warner and company returned in 1955 to capture their second straight Rucker Championship, turning back Snooky's once again. At that time, many of the great Harlem Rens were beginning to retire. With the Rens in decline, Snooky's coach John Walker leased the franchise from Bob Douglas, combined his roster with Ed Warner's, and went barnstorming under the name Young Rens.

The late Snooky Walker—his mother gave him that nickname when he was still in her arms—was recently described to me by his widow, Dolores Walker, as "the unofficial mayor of Harlem." He was a businessman who had met Holcombe Rucker through their mutual friend Ollie Edinboro. A man of small height but great stature, Snooky, like Holcombe, was a World War II veteran. He had earned a high school diploma at the elite Stuyvesant High School in the late 1930s and already owned two small restaurants in Harlem before joining the army. While serving Uncle Sam in Okinawa, he became an army chef.

After the war, Snooky came back to Harlem and to Dolores, his childhood sweetheart. He picked up where he had left off in the food business, opening up a few more eateries, including Snooky's Sugar Bowl on 137th Street and Seventh Avenue. Snooky's Sugar Bowl catered to nearby neighborhood churches now famous around the world, the Abyssinian Baptist Church and the Mother African Methodist Episcopal Zion Church, the first black church (1896) established in New York State.

A young minister named Adam Clayton Powell often ducked into Snooky's for a quick bite to eat, and the luncheonette became a hamburger hangout for neighborhood kids, many of whom were starring in Rucker's tournament, where basketball was being worshiped just a long bounce pass away.

"Snooky knew that all those young kids had girlfriends, and that they would be good for business," Dolores said. "He basically turned that luncheonette into a community center."

One day Ollie Edinboro walked into Snooky's place and asked if he'd be interested in sponsoring a team in Rucker's showcase, and Snooky, who had been a member of the swim team at Stuyvesant and played very little basketball, nevertheless said "Why not?" anyway.

"He became the owner and the coach," Dolores said. "He was very proud of that team."

Snooky and Holcombe fast became good friends, and through the years, as Snooky's wealth grew along with his many investments, he often donated money to help keep Rucker's vision afloat.

"With money from his own pockets, Snooky took those Renaissance teams on the road, and he took other all-black teams to compete upstate in the Catskills against all-white teams," Dolores said. "He was a great owner, and all of his players loved him."

Snooky's Young Rens played black and white teams alike around the country, many of the games against their white competition often ending in fistfights with opposing players and fans. And like the Harlem Rens and Chicago Bears before them, the new players soon found that traveling to some places outside New York City meant having to eat dinner on the team bus, as some white establishments would not serve them.

On the court, however, people who really knew and appreciated the game, especially white coaches, kept their eyes on those all-black teams in hopes of incorporating some of their strategy and style into their own playbooks. In fact, Isaacs insists that a young Red Auerbach, who would become the mastermind of the Boston Celtics dynasty, stole the motion offense he made famous in Beantown from the all-black Bears.

"If you really want to know who started the motion offense, the figure-eight, pass and go through, pass and go away, Red Auerbach would have you believe he did, but he's full of it," Isaacs said. "During the war, 1940, '41, and '42, he was stationed in Norfolk Naval, and every week, Red would come up from Norfolk with his petty officer's uniform on and watch us play at Turner's Arena in D.C.

"Red was there to count heads, because he knew sometimes we would split the team in half, some of us would go to New York and the other half would stay in Washington, and we'd need some local guys to fill the roster. Red always wanted to play, though he never did with the Bears. We were an all-black team, but that didn't mean nothing to Red, because the guy just loved the game. In that sense, he was no different from the rest of us."

The barnstorming team that Snooky Walker put together included a six five center who had moved to Harlem from Miami and had preceded Cal Ramsey at Commerce. The neighborhood kids had been calling Ronald Evans "Knowledge" ever since the day he made the fatal mistake of walking into a poolroom holding one of his favorite Mickey Spillane books, which he planned on reading while some of the older men played eight-ball.

On that day, a man in the poolroom began teasing young Ronald by snatching his book. He tossed it to a friend, who tossed it to another. Everyone laughed as Ronald's book circled the room, its pages fluttering in the smoky air. Then one man yelled, "Hey, this young guy is trying to get all the knowledge," and that's how his nickname was born.

"They were just trying to give me the business, trying to put me in my place," said Evans, now sixty-eight. "I guess I didn't know the rules, but from then on, I never brought another one of my books into a poolroom, and I learned in that room that if anybody messed with you, you had better be ready to fight back."

Evans, whose parents were from the West Indies, lost his mother in 1938, when she was just twenty-one years old and he was just four. Growing up in Harlem, a neighborhood filled with children living in single-parent households, Evans was thankful for additional role models like Holcombe Rucker and John "Snooky" Walker to lean on.

"These weren't park directors and league organizers who had some fancy office in New Rochelle," said Evans of Rucker and Walker. "These were guys who spent real time with kids, who went to the same barbershops, the same laundromats, and the same supermarkets we went to. These were guys who called you into the park to talk about basketball or whatever else was on your mind, and that was important to a kid like me, a kid who had grown up in West Indian communities and was in culture shock when he came to New York after seeing all the gangs and subways, and everything else I had never seen in a big city before.

"Holcombe, I loved him," Evans said. "He was a very enthusiastic, very gregarious, very exuberant individual."

In his two years at Commerce, 1952 and 1953, Evans, who teamed there with Jack Defares, was a marginal player. But the advice and experience Knowledge absorbed by mixing it up on Rucker's asphalt surface after his senior season at Commerce helped transform him into an all-conference player at Fayetteville University, a basketball power in the predominantly black Central Intercollegiate Athletic Association (CIAA). This was the place where many black basketball stars took their acts in the 1950s and '60s, when they were turned away from schools that preferred mostly white faces on their rosters. The conference also included Winston-Salem State, the CIAA school that produced Earl Monroe and so many other stars of that era.

"To have had a chance to see the best, to play with the best," said Evans, "taught me all those little things I needed to know to become a better player."

Though he never played professional basketball, Knowledge Evans went on to be that other kind of professional that the Pied Piper helped produce during his deeply meaningful time on this earth.

In New York City, Evans would become one of the first black teachers appointed principal directly from the classroom. As principal of the often-beleaguered Intermediate School 201 in Harlem, Evans helped oversee a controversial, four-year experiment in community control that made headlines around the Big Apple and beyond.

That experiment significantly increased the number of minority administrators and principals throughout a predominantly white school system, which in turn, Evans said at the time, affected the "backward educational slide" of the mostly poor black and Spanish-speaking student population.

"I understood the importance of the needy faces on the kids in my community," Knowledge Evans said. "Holcombe Rucker taught me that."

The Marquee Changes

With the top two pro teams combined into the barnstorming Young Rens and now missing from the tournament by 1956, it was time for a new cast of great players to create their legends on Rucker's stage, time for new teams to come along and battle for what had quickly become streetball's ultimate bragging rights.

The spotlight began to shift to the college and high school division games, where some of the biggest crowds at Rucker Park were gathering to cheer for Cal Ramsey and Satch Sanders, the college teammates at NYU who played for a college-division team called United Players Basketball Association (UPBA).

Ramsey, an all-city player at Commerce High on the Upper East Side, and Sanders, a product of Seward Park High School on the Lower East Side, led UPBA to three straight championships from 1957 through 1959.

Sanders, considered one of the NBA's best defensive forwards ever, turned out to be the better pro, but Ramsey was clearly the bigger star at Rucker Park. At six four, Ramsey was an astounding rebounder for a player his size, outclassing and outglassing much taller competition. He went on to play at NYU, where he averaged a whopping 19.6 rebounds per game in his sophomore season, a record that still stands. He then played professionally for the New York Knicks. Ramsey, in fact, is the answer to one

of the great trivia questions about the history of the fabled
league, as he is the only player to have won an MVP award at
the high school, college, and pro levels.

Ramsey is now an assistant basketball coach at NYU. He also
serves as director of special events and community relations for
the Knicks.

Ramsey said that for all he has accomplished in basketball, he
has Holcombe Rucker to thank.

"I too came from a single-parent household," he said. "We
moved from Alabama to Harlem when I was just eight years old,
and that's when I met the man. He was like a father figure.

"A lot of us would just go down to the park and sit around with
him and talk basketball. He was a terrific guy, very well liked, very
outgoing and easy to talk to," Ramsey said. "And by going back to
school, Holcombe Rucker practiced what he preached."

While Ramsey and Sanders were tag-teaming their way to
Rucker immortality, the Pied Piper continued his never-ending
search to fill his tournament with top-notch talent, sending ver-
bal invitations to quality players throughout New York's five boroughs. In fact, he had sent word down to the Lower East Side
in the summer of 1952 to a dazzling six-foot point guard named
Stanley Hill. When the young man got the Pied Piper's message,
he slung his sneakers over his scrawny shoulders and headed
uptown.

"Holcombe had a great personality, and he was a very sincere
man," said Hill. "I was just a kid, and I had never met him before, but I was comfortable around him in a matter of minutes.
I started teasing him about how the best ballplayers in New York
were from the Lower East Side, and he just laughed.

"He was the type of guy who loved helping kids, which is why he wanted me in his tournament. He wanted me and everyone else to play against the very best so that I could reach my full potential."

Hill, a high school all-American teammate of Cal Ramsey's on the great Commerce squad that went 37–0 in the 1954 regular season before losing to Stuyvesant in the first round of the PSAL playoffs that year, joined Ramsey and Satch Sanders in hoisting one of three Rucker championship trophies won by the UPBA in the late 1950s.

From 1951 through 1959, during which he starred at Commerce and at Iona College, Hill played in Rucker Park. He not only played but even reffed several games that the great Connie Hawkins played in.

"Half the time that Connie came down with the ball, I just swallowed my whistle and became a spectator," Hill said. "He did some spectacular things out there."

While most of those memories are priceless, there's one he prefers to forget.

"The one moment from the Rucker that stands out in my mind is the game in which Lonnie West of Wagner College went up for a rebound, came down in an awkward manner, and literally broke his leg in half," said Hill, who played in that game against West, a lanky six seven forward from Harlem. "It's been almost fifty years, but I can still hear the nasty sound of that break. I can still hear Lonnie screaming and crying in pain.

"Holcombe and the rest of us were so upset for Lonnie that day, we just stopped playing," Hill said. "We just went out and had a cup of coffee, and just kind of sat around and stared at each other."

The Rucker Tournament was a racial paradise for black play-

ers. But on January 2, 1957, Stanley Hill became a part of the
ugly side of basketball played in America in the years before the
civil rights movement. With Rucker Park blanketed in snow,
Hill and the rest of the Iona Gaels were in Owensboro, Kentucky, set to play the University of Mississippi in a holiday tournament game.

Minutes before the game, with most of the crowd already in
their seats and players from both teams just seconds away from
running out to their respective layup lines, a booming voice
blared over the public address system.

The PA announcer informed the crowd that James Coleman,
then-governor of Mississippi, forbade the team from playing
Iona simply because Hill's skin was black. Iona was awarded a
forfeit victory.

"I was so embarrassed, so devastated," said Hill, the only
black player on that Iona team. "I'll never forget the impact it
had on me and my family. Someone told me that Holcombe got
wind of it, too, and that he wasn't very happy about it."

That same night, Hill was visited by the Mississippi coach
and the rest of the Rebel players, all of whom apologized for
Governor Coleman's disorderly conduct.

"That was a nice gesture on their part," Hill said. "It put me
a little more at ease."

Forty-four long years later, a basketball script that Holcombe
Rucker would have been proud to write was played out in
Kansas City, Missouri, where Iona and Mississippi were meeting
in the 2001 NCAA tournament.

Before that game—won by Mississippi 72–70—Hill posed for
pictures with the Rebels, and he was presented with an auto-
graphed ball.

"My wife and I were hounded that whole weekend, but we loved every minute of it," said Hill, now sixty-six and living in Queens. "You can't erase history, but you can erase some of the pain that history has caused."

Like Ronald "Knowledge" Evans before him, Stanley Hill became yet another impact player who leaped off Holcombe Rucker's roster and into the national spotlight. But Stanley Hill's arena was a political one, and in November 1986 he rose to become the first black leader of the 115,000-member District Council 37, the largest union of municipal employees in New York.

On November 27, 1986, Michael Oreskes of the *New York Times* wrote that Hill's historic post "instantly puts him at the center of the city's interwoven worlds of labor, government and politics."

And like Ronald "Knowledge" Evans and scores of New York City kids before and after him, Stanley Hill says he has the Pied Piper to thank for everything in life that he became, and everything in life that he did not become.

"Holcombe didn't believe in just coming to the park, putting in his time, and going home," Hill said. "When one of us needed him, he was right there, right where we could find him. He had those special qualities, the ability to teach and educate, and if he felt he could help you, he'd seek you out, just like he did with me. The last thing he wanted was for one of us to end up on the streets and in trouble."

Hill, whose first jobs after graduating from Iona were as a caseworker helping troubled kids and working as an organizer for youth basketball leagues, patterned his personal style after Harlem's mentor.

"I had the same kind of philosophy as Holcombe," Hill said. "I made sure that the kids who played for me went to school and were getting good grades, and I tried to bring to those kids the same kind of dedication and commitment that Holcombe brought to us.

"And when I started working with union people, I tried to bring the same kind of organization and quiet yet effective leadership that Holcombe brought to the overall structuring of his great league.

"It was only then," said Hill, "that I realized just how hard Holcombe's job really was, and just how easy and effortless he made it all look. In every sense of the word, the man was a legend."

A Giant Invasion

One weekend each summer, Rucker would arrange for his best college and pro players to compete against visiting teams from Philadelphia. In the summer of 1957, three dynamic players from Temple University in Philly named Hal "King" Lear, Guy Rodgers, and Jay Norman came north to do battle with Ramsey, Sanders, and a host of other hoop magicians from the Big Apple, including Nurlin Terrant, a backcourt man from Brooklyn who starred at Thomas Jefferson High School before moving on to Lincoln University in Missouri, and fellow Brooklynite Dick "Chink" Gaines, who starred at Franklin K. Lane and made a name for himself at Seton Hall University.

Rodgers, six-foot nothing, had a brilliant twelve-year NBA career in which he made four all-star appearances and left his mark as perhaps the greatest passing small-man professional hoops has ever known.

Though Lear played only one season in the NBA, Norman said the King "was one of the greatest shooters" he had ever seen. It was King Lear who put up the biggest numbers in the consolation game of the 1956 NCAA Final Four, the championship won that season by San Francisco–led Bill Russell, which defeated Iowa.

Against Southern Methodist University, Lear, a deadly shooter from eighteen to twenty feet, poured in 48 points, a record that stood for years until broken by Bill Bradley. Despite the fact that he did not wear a championship crown that season, the King still walked off with the Final Four's MVP award.

Lear and company brought a ringer to Rucker's park in 1957. This was not some little-known pro playing in the Eastern League, or some hotshot NBA rookie granted special permission to play. This ringer happened to be the most ballyhooed high school player in the country, Wilt Chamberlain. The seven-foot-one-and-one-sixteenth-inch man-child from Philly's Overbrook High School, who had not yet gone off to play at Kansas, terrorized the New York collegians in a game won by Philly.

"Even Wilt knew he had to be on top of his game to play with our backcourt of Guy Rodgers and Hal 'King' Lear," said Norman. "I consider them to be the best guard tandem in the history of college basketball."

This was Chamberlain's first taste of Rucker action, the kind of action that the basketball behemoth would return for numerous times throughout his remarkable career.

"To see Cal and Wilt go head-to-head in those days was quite something," said William "Billy The Kid" Baxter, who saw the two do battle as a kid growing up in Harlem and later became an outstanding playmaker and ball handler who played with a team called the Rucker Pros in the 1960s and early '70s.

Roger Gibbs, another Commerce star who would later team with Chamberlain and Ramsey in Rucker's pro division—the threesome would tool around Manhattan in the Big Dipper's (Chamberlain's) bright red Oldsmobile convertible back in those days—remembers what Chamberlain did to Ramsey in that all-star game.

"Wilt dunked on Cal—from the foul line," Gibbs said. "I remember telling myself at the time that it wasn't possible, but I had to believe it because I had just seen it."

Though Billy Baxter attended Commerce High School from 1955 to 1958, he never played there, opting instead to take an after-school job as a messenger to help his father support the family.

"I elected not to play on the team," said Baxter, who is now sixty-one and lives in Englewood, New Jersey. "My parents struggled financially while raising four children, and I didn't want my father under so much strain."

Despite not playing at Commerce, Baxter still played his summer ball at Rucker Park, and a year before he would go off to college, Holcombe Rucker got his pen out, and on that weathered green bench that served as his office chair, began drafting letters of recommendation on Baxter's behalf to a number of his college basketball contacts, just as he had done for so many other kids in need of a shove in the right direction. Eventually, Baxter was off to play at St. Augustine's College in Raleigh, North Carolina, where he would team in the backcourt for four seasons with Brooklyn's Al Glover, a shooting guard who had starred at Franklin K. Lane.

"That's the kind of influence Mr. Rucker had, and the kind of reputation his tournament had," Baxter said. "He was able to send a kid like me to play college ball without anyone having seen me play at the high school level, because the people he contacted trusted his evaluations and assessments of the players he had known. Even those people around the country who didn't know Mr. Rucker personally respected the man from a distance."

Baxter never played pro ball, but for thirty-seven years he followed the Pied Piper's path, working with the New York City Parks and Recreation Department. He still officiates at high school basketball games.

"He inspired me to go into that line of work," Baxter said. "I knew I could never do all the things for kids that Holcombe Rucker did, but I'd like to think I've done my part."

Billy The Kid was involved in one of the most memorable, and certainly embarrassing, plays at Rucker's Park on 130th Street and Seventh Avenue, though he was not the player who went home blushing. That dubious privilege went to a crafty five eleven guard from Harlem named Lou "Louie Orlaski" Huston.

During an open-tournament game in the summer of 1958, Louie Orlaski, playing on a team called the Local Yocals, came to run and gun against Billy The Kid. He did not know, however, that The Kid was covered from the rooftops by a skywalking small forward named Butch Vaughn, who played his college ball at Central State in Ohio and ran with the Kid's Rucker team from Long Island called Woodmere.

"I told Mr. Rucker I was going to take it hard to the hole against The Kid," said Louie Orlaski, who earned his nickname by hanging out with his Italian paisanos from East Harlem. "But Mr. Rucker had warned me about Vaughn, about how he loved to embarrass people by swatting their shots out of the air."

For the first, and last, time in his life, Louie Orlaski didn't listen to the Pied Piper's advice. Early in the game, Mr. Orlaski, as advertised, went hard at Billy The Kid. The capacity crowd held its collective breath as The Kid stepped up to the foul line to play some hard D. The two players met there, and as The Kid reached for Louie Orlaski's handle, Orlaski spun on him, nearly breaking The Kid's ankles. The crowd roared in approval as Louie Orlaski motored down the lane, holding the ball high in the air as if Wilson itself were the head of Billy The Kid on a platter.

As he stormed to the tin, Orlaski rose high and let loose a soft floater he intended on banking off the backboard. As soon as the ball left Orlaski's fingertips, Vaughn came cheetah-fast from the weak side, rising to meet his prey in midflight. Somewhere very high above the cylinder, Vaughn, palm out, threw his right arm behind his back, almost using a pitcher-like windup to gain momentum, and then let his arm whip forward in slingshot fashion to swat Orlaski's shot attempt. Vaughn's timing was perfect. He swatted the ball clear OUT of the park and onto Seventh Avenue.

"I never saw the block," Orlaski said. "All I remember was seeing the soles of Vaughn's sneakers soaring over my head."

As the ball danced between heavy traffic, hundreds of spectators spilled onto the court to congratulate Vaughn for turning Orlaski's shot into a total eclipse of the mind.

"People were literally falling out of the trees," Huston said. "Mr. Rucker ran onto the court and grabbed me. He knew I felt kind of bad. He just smiled a little and said, 'Lou, I told you that boy could get up there, you should have listened to me.' "

The Bronx versus Brooklyn

While the college and high school games sizzled, other pro teams were starting to assert themselves by decade's end. A team calling themselves the Bronx All-Stars wore the 1958 and 1959 pro division crowns. The Bronx All-Stars were coached by a park legend named Ted Jones, who starred at Samuel Gompers High School in the mid-1940s but never played college ball.

"Every year I prayed that we would get into the finals because I wanted to be a part of that whole scene," Jones said. "It was the next best thing to playing in Madison Square Garden, and all them people hanging in the trees, I always looked at them like they were fans watching from the Garden balcony.

"Let me tell you how important winning that tournament was at that time," Jones said. "If you wanted a million dollars back then but couldn't get it, winning a Rucker championship was the next best thing. As a player and a coach, I never wanted to be anywhere else."

The Bronx contingent was led by scandal-scarred Floyd Layne, who had found the same kind of love and forgiveness that Rucker fans had given to his City College teammate Ed Warner.

Layne saddled up for competition with the Durango Kid, otherwise known as Ralph Bacote, a smooth-shooting six three guard who played at Morris High School in the Bronx before taking his game to Northern Illinois in the mid-1950s. Bacote's nickname was born out of his shooting style, which he patterned after then–New York Knick Carl Braun. Bacote shot from the hip, just like Braun, and just like the old television cowboy Charles Starrett, who played the Durango Kid. Bacote, now head basketball coach at the Bronx School of Science, was also notorious for shooting baskets by himself in the dark, putting in the extra work beneath the watchful eye of a Harlem moon.

The Bronx roster also featured gifted big-man Ray Felix, the former Long Island University star and longtime pro who was then playing for the New York Knicks. Felix, now deceased, is best remembered not for what he did in Holcombe Rucker's tournament, but for what the six eleven, 220-pound center did to Mr. Rucker himself during a basketball clinic in the summer of 1954. He knocked out the Pied Piper's two front teeth during a rebounding drill.

"Our biggest rival back then was Brooklyn USA," Bacote said. "Jackie Jackson, Eddie Simmons, and Bruce Spraggins, man, they don't make players like that anymore."

"Jumping" Jackie Jackson, Eddie "The Czar" Simmons, and Bruce "Prom Boy" Spraggins, fan favorites at Rucker Park, were all teammates at Virginia Union. Jumping Jackie, whose phenomenal leaping ability accounted for his nickname, stormed into the national spotlight in the late 1950s while he was still in college.

Spraggins grew up in small-town Williamsburg, Virginia, and his New York nickname was Prom Boy because everything he saw in the big city simply wowed him. He vividly remembers a Holiday Invitational game at Madison Square Garden versus CIAA rival Johnson C. Smith University in Charlotte.

The moment is still frozen in time. A Johnson player puts up a shot that misses. The six five Spraggins rips the ball off the boards and outlets to the Czar in transition. The Czar finds Jumping Jackie just above half-court with a chest pass and stays on his wing. Jumping Jackie steam-dribbles forward as a Johnson defender positions himself just inside the free throw line.

"Everybody in the gym is waiting for Jackie to pull up," Spraggins said. "But the son of a gun keeps going."

Jumping Jackie stormed toward the foul line as the defender braced himself for a charge. Sensing impact, the defender closed his eyes. He shouldn't have though, because he was the only player in the house who missed what happened next.

"Jackie leaps over the guy, I mean over his head, and the guy's about six feet tall," Spraggins said. "Jackie clears the guy's head, glides in midair to the hoop, and throws it down.

"I've never seen anything like it," said Spraggins, still shaking his head in disbelief a half century later. "Everybody just freaked out."

So did the kid Jumping Jackie leaped over, a player named Curly Neal, who, along with Meadowlark Lemon, Marques Haynes, and Goose Tatum would become the most famous of all Harlem Globetrotters.

"What can I say?" is how Jackson describes his unusual relationship with gravity. "I was one bad dude back then."

Racism Still a Part of the Game

As Stanley Hill's experience in Kentucky so sadly illustrates, the 1950s was a time when segregation and racial discrimination were still rearing their ugly heads all over the country. The great color divide that baseball's Jackie Robinson had so courageously confronted and broken the decade before still cut right through the heart of the basketball world, denying young black men an opportunity to compete against their white counterparts, and vice versa, hurting the sport most at the top collegiate and professional levels.

Richard "Skinny" Reed, a Rucker alum who starred at all-black Benedict College in South Carolina from 1953 to 1957, remembers Benedict scrimmaging with the University of South Carolina, an all-white school with an all-white team in the days before Frank McGuire took over the program.

"We played every one of those scrimmages on our home court, early on Saturday mornings," said Reed, a six one guard who went to Benedict after a stellar career at Central Needle Trade High School, now called Fashion Institute.

"We couldn't run the risk of playing on the South Carolina campus because the police there would have locked us up," Reed said. "The South Carolina players always felt bad about it, but all of us knew that's just the way life was in those days. None of us liked it, but we had to live with it. In fact, when players from either school wanted to get together socially, we'd throw secret parties off campus in heavily wooded areas, away from those blaring police lights and sirens."

Reed, now seventy-two, was one of Holcombe Rucker's first assistants in the parks, working as a referee and scorekeeper when he got back from the Marine Corps in 1953, the summer before he would leave for Benedict.

"This man did so much with so little," Reed said of Holcombe. "He'd pay me for a full day's work in the park with a soda, and you know what, I appreciated it because I knew that was all he could afford to pay me."

But Reed, like every other Harlem kid who came into contact with their playground mentor, also knew that just being around Rucker always paid dividends. The Pied Piper was always there to lend a listening ear, always there to offer words of advice or encouragement after local kids brought tales of discrimination, corruption, scandal, racism, or their own neighborhood violence to their home away from home.

Reed remembers Rucker just shaking his head after Reed had relayed another story about the Benedict players in the summer of 1958. Still on campus taking summer courses, Reed and a bunch of his teammates felt it was a bit too warm and uncomfortable shooting hoops at their home gymnasium, so they ventured up the road a bit to an all-white Bible-study school that had an outdoor court on its property. The Benedict crew and several other players from the Bible school chose up sides, went shirts and skins, and got it going.

Minutes later, the wail of police sirens found them again.

"Put your shirts on, boys," one police officer told them, "and get the hell out of here!"

Reed looked north and thought about an old friend.

"One of the only places where black and white kids could play ball in peace together was at the Rucker," he said. "I mean, as far as black and white players went, we were only interested in playing a game we all loved."

It was Reed, in fact, who brought one of the first white teams to Rucker Park, a roster filled with Jewish kids from Manhattan whom Reed had met while working on construction sites with the Lower East Side Laborers Association.

Neil Goldstein, a dynamic five eight point guard from Seward Park High School and one of the few white kids who hung with, and starred among, black athletes in those days, was one of Reed's Laborers who played in the collegiate division before Rucker's predominantly black crowds. Goldstein, who now runs a trophy manufacturing company in Manhattan, played on the Laborers with his Seward Park teammate Charlie "The Pipe"

Levitz, a five eight forward whose nickname didn't reflect his big, strong game as much as his prominent nose. They were joined by a Russian kid named Sam Proneick, a five ten forward who had teamed with Freddie Crawford at Samuel Gompers in the Bronx.

"As long as you had a game, you were treated like royalty at Rucker Park," said Goldstein, now sixty-two. "The color of your skin had nothing to do with how you were treated up there, at least not where we were concerned. I don't think any one of us ever felt threatened.

"Don't forget, we were Jewish kids," Goldstein said. "At that time, we knew exactly what black ballplayers were going through in terms of discrimination, because we were going through it as well."

Indeed, Goldstein would learn firsthand what black players like Skinny Reed were feeling at that time. In the fall of 1960, Goldstein would go to play his college ball, or try to, at Southern Mississippi, where black players, like the hundreds he had competed with and against on the New York City streets, were simply not accepted.

"And right below blacks on their hate list were Jews and northerners," Goldstein said. "I fell into both categories, so it was murder for me at that place. No matter where I went, all I heard people say was 'Yankee go home.' Being white and Jewish up in Harlem was a breeze compared to that."

Goldstein, who redshirted his first season at the school under head coach Fred Lewis, remembered some students hanging and burning Lewis in effigy after the coach said publicly that he'd prefer adding black players to his roster.

"It nearly caused a riot," Goldstein said. "These were igno-rant, backward people who played 'Dixie' before they sang the national anthem, and most of the players on that team were big, dumb white boys who had gotten thrown out of every school they ever attended."

Lewis, it turned out, got the last laugh. The coach moved on to Syracuse in 1962, turning the Orangemen into a national powerhouse with star black players like Vaughn Harper and Dave Bing, who would become an NBA Hall of Famer.

"When Coach Lewis left, I dropped out," Goldstein said. "I never got to play a single minute of basketball there, and I really didn't care." Goldstein never played a minute of college basketball after that anywhere in the United States. He returned to New York and found a job as a gym director with the Boys Club of New York, working there for a year before moving on to the trophy manufacturing business.

Racial discrimination also stalked Jackie Jackson, Ed Simmons, and Bruce Spraggins of Virginia Union in the early summer following the 1958–59 college basketball season. All three had gone to visit their friend Jeff Cohen, a white all-American player at the College of William and Mary in Williamsburg, Virginia.

Cohen, who would go on to play professionally with the Hawaii Chiefs of the old American Basketball League and later in the American Basketball Association, had heard about Virginia Union's Big Three, who were wowing crowds just fifty-two miles away in Richmond. Cohen knew all about Jackson, the only player in the nation, and in the world, capable of snatching quarters and fifty-cent pieces off the tops of backboards.

"During practice we used to run a drill where we would make two layup lines, and with an imaginary ball in our hands, go to the hoop for layups," said Gibbs, one of Jackson's teammates at

Virginia Union. "The purpose of the drill was to get guys accus-
tomed to getting as high as they could above the rim, so that
when the ball was actually in their hands, they could elevate to
the max and find a comfortable release point.

"Whenever we ran that drill, everyone just stopped and stared
at Jackie," Gibbs said. "He would get up so high, he'd be able to
rest both of his elbows on the rim. It was one of the most incredible things I have ever seen on a basketball court."

Cohen and Gibbs were in such awe of Jumping Jackie, they
even carried in their wallets the "business" card Jackson gave to
them and to anyone who would take it from him in those days.
HAVE CONVERSE, WILL JUMP were the only words written on Jumping Jackie's card, because, as Jackson liked to say, he "was all
about the business of playing basketball."

So was Cohen, who in 1961 would become one of the few
white players to tour with the Harlem Globetrotters. Cohen
scored 2,003 points at William and Mary and remains The
Tribe's career-leading rebounder with 1,679. The six seven
power forward, who died in 1978 after battling cancer, is best remembered for outdueling West Virginia's Jerry West in a classic
1960 contest in which he scored 36 points to help The Tribe put
an end to West Virginia's fifty-six-game winning streak.

While that game made headlines around the nation, Jackson
said few people know about a different kind of day Jeff Cohen
spent on the hardwood, that same day when Jumping Jackie,
Simmons, and Spraggins were visiting Cohen on the William
and Mary campus. They were there to shoot some hoops with a
friend they had made through basketball, and to ask Cohen if
he'd be interested in joining their Brooklyn USA squad in the
Rucker Tournament. Cohen, they felt, would be the perfect answer to Ray Felix of the Bronx All-Stars.

As the four players horsed around on a quiet afternoon, the gymnasium doors suddenly burst wide open and campus police, guns drawn, stormed the court.

"What's up?" Jackson asked.

"You know what's up," Jackson remembers one of the campus cops telling him. The cop lifted his nightstick to make a point: "No black players allowed in the gym, period," he said.

"Jeff was so upset," Jackson said. "We told him not to worry, that we were used to stuff like that, but Jeff kept mouthing off to the police.

"Then the cops began to chastise Jeff," said Jackson. "They told him that he should have known better than to bring niggers on campus. Jeff was so damned embarrassed by the whole thing."

Two weeks after the incident at William and Mary, Jeff Cohen was in New York battling Ray Felix on Rucker soil. Spectators and participants remember both players fighting to a standstill, the tight game ultimately decided by the Durango Kid, who went for 30 from the hip, giving the Bronx All-Stars back-to-back crowns.

After shooting the lights out, the Durango Kid rode off into the sunset, waving his MVP trophy until he disappeared in the distance.

"Brooklyn had such a great team," said Bacote, "but they kept running into an awful lot of talent in the finals."

Those Other Redmen

As the 1950s were coming to a close, another Jewish kid, Mel Feldman, was coaching a high school team at Rucker Park that included a pair of rising young black players from the Bronx named Nevil "The Shadow" Shed, who was on his way to Morris High School, and Gene Feaster, about to attend DeWitt Clinton. Feaster asked Feldman one afternoon if he could bring his cousin Johnny out to play with their team, nicknamed the Redmen. Johnny, a kid from Georgia, had been visiting Nevil's family that summer.

"Can he play?" Feldman asked Feaster.

"Yeah, he's pretty good," Feaster replied.

With Johnny Mathis on their side, Feldman's Redmen would become one of the top schoolboy attractions at the park. Mathis, whom Feldman said learned a lot of his moves up at the Ruck, would later become a star at Savannah State, and the six seven forward played the 1967–68 season with the New Jersey Americans of the ABA.

Feldman's Redmen had gained fame in the eyes of Rucker Park fans and throughout the playgrounds of New York City for what they had achieved during a game in the summer of 1959 at the Ray Felix Tournament in Elmhurst, Queens. The Ray Felix Tournament, an offshoot of the Rucker Tournament, was sponsored by Felix as a way of giving back to the Pied Piper and the rest of the community.

Since Nevil, Feaster, and Mathis were not available, Feldman had on his roster Eddie Simmons of Brooklyn and two other Bronx kids, Bruce Moody and Walt "Doc" Holiday.

In perhaps the most famous contest ever played in the Ray Felix tourney, the Redmen squared off against another Rucker power, Snooky's Sugar Bowl, and the team's star six eight center, Stretch Dawson.

On that day the Redmen brought only five players, and when their two white players, Vinnie Kempton, who had gone to St. Joseph's, and Jerry Glenn, a six ten center from Yale, had fouled out, the Redmen were left to play Snooky's three against five.

"Eddie said, don't worry, let's play a three-man zone," said Moody, who is sixty-two and now lives in Georgia. "I rebounded, Doc shot, and Eddie did the rest."

Despite playing an entire half two men short, the threesome wowed a large crowd by dominating Snooky's.

"Simmons was dribbling right through guys," Feldman said. "Four guys on Snooky's fouled out just trying to stop him, but they couldn't."

It was in this game, won by the Redmen, that Eddie Simmons earned the nickname Czar. "At least on that one day," said Feldman, "in front of all those people, Eddie Simmons was king of all point guards."

A few years later, Moody, one of the all-time greats at Marshall University, who encountered his own share of racism, remembers walking past a fan in the stands at West Virginia State before a game between the two schools. Just before Moody joined the layup line, a fan shouted in his direction.

"Hey, you're one of those three guys that beat Snooky's that day in Queens!" the fan shouted. "Greatest game I've ever seen!"

Although Mathis was the only Redman to make it to the NBA, Nevil Shed and two other Rucker alums from the Bronx, Willie Wursley of DeWitt Clinton and Arnold Cager of Morris High School, would later become more famous as members of the 1966 Texas Western basketball team that defeated the seemingly invincible Kentucky Wildcats and their legendary coach, Adolph Rupp, for the NCAA championship. That game marked the first time an all-white starting five—which included a young hotshot named Pat Riley—met an all-black starting five in the NCAA.

Nevil and company, household names only in their own

households, knocked off the highly favored and nationally recognized Cats 72–65. This was no fluke, as Texas Western proved faster, quicker, and more skilled. That one game is generally credited with accelerating integration in the South.

"Nevil always played with a tremendous amount of heart," Moody said. "Like all of us playing at Rucker Park, he was learning how to use his wings to soar to higher places."

The Eccentric Spook

While white players like Jeff Cohen, Neil Goldstein, and Mel Feldman felt comfortable playing before thousands of mostly black fans at Holcombe Rucker's games, the Rucker faithful did ruffle the feathers of a white, eccentric, and lovable basketball character named Freddie "Spook" Stegman, who coached several all-white teams at Rucker Tournament games in the late 1950s and early 1960s.

A talent scout who had been combing the five boroughs since the mid-1940s, Spook was largely responsible for piping quality New York City stars to the legendary Al McGuire at Belmont Abbey in North Carolina, and he loved bringing his all-white squad into the fabled park to play against Rucker's predominantly black superstars.

The Spook, whose claim to fame in those years was that every Division I college coach in America had his phone number, was a street agent of sorts who made a living cashing discreet paychecks from college coaches whose rosters shined with kids the Spook had steered in their direction.

Belmont Abbey was a small school of a thousand students run by the order of St. Benedict monks in Belmont, North Carolina (population 5,000), a textile town eight miles west of Charlotte.

In his first season at Belmont Abbey, McGuire, who had inherited a team that finished 4–25 the season before, finished 24–3 with players that Spook Stegman helped steer his way. These were gritty New York players like Danny "Sunshine" Doyle, a six eight forward from Queens, and John von Bargen, a six ten center from Mount Vernon, New York. Before long, nearby Division I powers North Carolina, North Carolina State, and Duke wanted no part of playing McGuire's team.

The Spook continued to steer players to McGuire, even after the coach landed at Marquette, where he won the national championship in the 1976–77 season.

"I'm from a lost era," said Spook, now seventy-four. "I'm from a time when kids, black and white alike, played ball for the love of the game. It's all about business now."

The fact that many players and spectators referred to Stegman's teams as simply "Spook's All-Stars" did not sit well with some fans in attendance, especially with integration still on shaky legs in the college and pro ranks.

But no matter how irate fans were at the sight of Spook's All-Stars, it was difficult to stay angry very long with Spook himself, a comical and charming sight along the sidelines. Spook, a disheveled bachelor with a number of teeth missing from his crooked smile, always took drastic measures to avoid getting sick. Even on those scorching, sun-drenched afternoons at Holcombe Rucker's place, he wore long johns beneath his trousers and a tan raincoat. Three or four times a week he'd pace the sidelines wearing the same blue shirt and blue-striped tie under the raincoat.

"Spook was quite a character," said Cal Ramsey. "He's the type of guy who's awfully hard to forget."

Stegman's Spooks were made up of a bunch of local boys including Tom Kearns, who helped North Carolina win the 1957 NCAA championship, defeating Big Wilt's Kansas squad in triple overtime that year. North Carolina coach Frank McGuire (no relation to Al), knowing he would lose the opening tip of that game to the Big Dipper, had the five eleven Kearns jump center against the seven one Chamberlain just for the heck of it.

"Having me, perhaps the smallest guy on the team, jump center against Wilt was probably more a psychological ploy than anything else," said Kearns, who recently made a basketball comeback of sorts by appearing in the Sean Connery movie *Finding Forrester*. "I remember Wilt not being very happy about it, either."

Kearns's Rucker Park career lasted a whole lot longer than his NBA career. He played seven minutes with Syracuse in the 1958–59 season, taking one shot from the field—and hitting it.

Kearns was cut from the Syracuse squad by player-coach Paul Seymour in favor of The King, Rucker alum Hal Lear. "Paul wanted to keep both of us," said Kearns, but the team's owner, Danny Biasone, said it made more financial sense at the time to retain the services of Lear and the less-expensive Seymour as players on his roster, and jettison Kearns.

But the kid who shot 1.000 with the Nats would do a lot better in the world of finance when his playing days ended, and in a new arena, he and the great Chamberlain would become teammates.

"Years later, Tommy handled Wilt's money, and I mean millions of dollars," the Spook said. "Wilt trusted Tommy, and the two became real good friends."

Indeed, the two men who had that strange encounter in the jump-circle stayed in touch, even took in a few Rucker games together throughout the years, and when Kearns became an all-star investor at Bear Stearns, Chamberlain played ball with him.

"I handled some of Wilt's finances," Kearns said. "At first I was a bit reluctant to cross that line with a friend, but I would pick my spots with him in terms of investing. Besides, Wilt had a lawyer out in Los Angeles who really looked out for him."

Kearns, who grew up in the Grand Concourse section of the Bronx and played his high school basketball at St. Ann's under a then-little-known coach named Lou Carnesecca, often traveled in hoop circles with fellow Bronxite Donnie Walsh, now the president of the Indiana Pacers, and Jack Magee, who went on to become the head coach at Georgetown before he was succeeded by a towel-toting genius named John Thompson.

The trio's constant searches for the big games usually took them to the Pied Piper's neck of the woods, where the Spook was always working the sidelines, always getting into the ears of kids he was trying to steer to certain colleges as favors to certain coaches.

"In those days, Spook ingratiated himself with a lot of people," Kearns said. "Spook was a little bit of a con man, always a little bit out of control, but he was all right once you learned not to take him too seriously."

Spook's All-Stars also featured Bo Erias, a star at Niagara University who played briefly with Minnesota of the NBA, and Donald Lane, a star at Dayton.

Stegman, now retired and living in Manhattan, admits to being intimidated playing before the all-black crowds.

"Hey, in those days, not too far from Rucker playground, they were preaching 'Be Black, Stay Black,' " Stegman said. "So for us to be going into that park and playing in front of all those black people was like going into Bensonhurst and not being Italian."

But Spook and company went anyway.

"Hey, we were all nervous at first, but it was still the best place in the world to play ball," he said. "And in the end, for a bunch of white guys to have been accepted by the brothers up there was just a wonderful feeling."

Another white star who played for the Spook was a tough Irish kid from Astoria, Queens, named Danny "Sunshine" Doyle, the powerfully built forward who played for Al McGuire at Belmont Abbey and fought through injuries to play four games with the Detroit Pistons during the 1962–63 season before deciding, "Screw the NBA, I could make more money delivering bottles on a Coca-Cola route in the off-season ($7,500) than I could playing a full pro basketball season ($6,500) back then."

At Rucker Park, Sunshine Doyle, who also played in the Eastern League, was the white kid with the biggest set of balls. He was white, and yes, he could dunk, and after flushing a fool or two on the hallowed blacktop, Doyle would run up and down the court "like a clown," declaring himself "king of Rucker Park" and shouting to anyone who cared to listen, "Nobody can stop me! Nobody can hold me!"

And after each game, the king of Queens would race to 125th Street to catch a bus back home, fearing someone might be in the mood to kick his behind after one of his little performances. Racing for that bus, Sunshine set record times in the mile and a half.

Doyle, who shared the same penchant for boozing and gambling as the Spook did back in their glory days, remembers getting tapped on the shoulder one night while shooting craps in a schoolyard near his home.

"I look up, and it's the Spook," said the sixty-three-year-old Doyle, whose son, Tim, now plays at St. John's. "I said, 'Spook, what the hell are you doing here?'

"Spook says to me, 'I brought Al McGuire to your house. He's talking to your parents, trying to get them to send you to Belmont Abbey. Better get your behind home right now.'

"I said, 'Spook, I'm going to North Carolina. Now get the hell outta here, I'm on a roll.'"

But as always, Spook Stegman got his man. He and McGuire somehow convinced Doyle's parents that their tough son, a hoops star at Bryant High School, would be better off attending Belmont Abbey, where half the student population was studying to become monks, than that basketball factory down Tobacco Road. And just like that, Danny "Sunshine" Doyle became Al McGuire's first big-time college recruit.

"Al was so happy with Spook, he bought him a new set of teeth," Doyle said. "No sense in giving the guy any money. He would have squandered it all away drinking or gambling. But all the smart coaches knew they needed Spook, so they always took care of him one way or another."

How Spook Stegman earned his nickname is the stuff of legend in a very prestigious basketball circle. One night in Rockaway, Queens, a New York City cop named Johnny McGuire was serving drinks from behind the bar he owned in the neighborhood where the McGuire boys, Johnny, Al, and Dick, at that time an all-star guard with the New York Knicks, had grown up.

McGuire's Bar and Grill, on 108th Street and Rockaway Boulevard, was less than a hundred yards from the ocean and from the park where some of the best three-on-three basketball games the world has ever known were being played. There, the McGuire brothers took on three-man teams that included the likes of Bob Cousy and his Boston Celtic teammate Tom Heinsohn, both of whom played their college ball at Holy Cross; Bobby Wanzer of Seton Hall and the Rochester Royals; and Ray Lumpp of NYU and the New York Knicks.

A number of black stars from the Rucker League often made hoop pilgrimages to Rockaway over the years. Players like Sherman White, Chink Gaines, Carl Green, and Jack Defares would knock down shots by day in the park, then knock down shots by night at McGuire's.

"Every Irish player that ever played basketball went in there up until 1965," said Danny Doyle. "It was a place that was ahead of its time in terms of sports bars and hanging out. We watched games there, drank, and talked sports between trips to the beach."

On Freddie Stegman night in Rockaway, the superscout would be at McGuire's doing what he usually did best at watering holes.

"You'd buy a drink for two bucks and put a ten-spot on the bar," said Doyle. "Then all of a sudden, you'd look back down and your eight dollars was suddenly four dollars, and then you'd look up, and there was Spook, yapping away with a drink in his hand that he bought off someone else's money."

With Stegman the barfly buzzing in Johnny McGuire's ear all night, McGuire got a little fed up, wheeled around, and lashed out at Stegman: "Ya know, you're like a goddamn spook," McGuire shouted. "You're like one of those damned ghosts who keep haunting people everywhere they turn." The name stuck.

While the Spook scored with Sunshine Doyle and a number of other city stars, he still laments the two biggest fish he let wiggle off his recruiting hook.

"I was hot on the trail of Connie Hawkins and Roger Brown," the Spook said. "Along with Lewie [Lew Alcindor], these were the greatest ballplayers ever to come out of New York City. I was trying to get both of them to attend Seattle University, but both of them got away—that was two tough pills to swallow."

Chapter 3

THE HAWK AND COMPANY
SWOOP IN

On a sunny afternoon in 1960, Rucker realized his tournament had outgrown the park at 130th Street and Seventh Avenue, where he was stationed by the Department of Parks as a recreational supervisor.

That day a couple of young Brooklynites named Connie Hawkins and Roger Brown, considered by many to be the two best high school basketball players in the country, were scheduled to do battle on the asphalt. Both were on hand to represent their borough in a high school division game.

The Hawk, as young Connie was known, was a tremendous rebounder and prolific scorer who had already received his share of ink in the city's sports pages, having led Boys High of Brooklyn to the first of back-to-back Public Schools Athletic League titles in 1959.

Lou Carnesecca, then an assistant coach at St. John's, paid a scouting visit to a 1959 game between Thomas Jefferson and Boys High and saw Hawkins, in one seamless display, block a Jefferson shot, knocking the ball all the way to midcourt, then lead the scramble for the ball, tipping it to the opponents' foul line, where he scooped it up and soared to the basket for a mighty slam.

"I ran out of the gym and didn't come back," Carnesecca said.

Brown, who made his bones at Wingate in Brooklyn, was an off-court friend and on-court rival of the high-flying Hawk during their schoolboy days. He was a fluid six five guard in an era when anyone over six two was put under the basket and told to stay there.

Both players would meet in a 1960 PSAL playoff game widely considered one of the all-time classics. Boys High won the game, but the smaller Brown outscored the six-foot-eight-inch Hawkins 39–18, forcing the Hawk to foul out in the third period. A senior in 1960, Brown would break the PSAL scoring mark of 1,433 points established by Tony Jackson of Thomas Jefferson, another of Rucker's high school stars. Brown averaged 25 points per game as a senior, finishing his career with a then-PSAL record of 1,574 points.

Days before their arrival at Rucker Park, word began to spread throughout Harlem. By 10 A.M. that morning, thousands of spectators had already squeezed into the tiny park. Triple-parked cars could be seen five or six blocks away from the site, and even police on patrol parked their cars and scooters to try to sneak a peek at the two players.

By the time Hawkins and Brown arrived at the park that afternoon, there was barely enough room for them to play one-on-one. The court was virtually reduced to the size of a bowling lane.

Rucker had no choice but to cancel the game. Policemen ringing the park used bullhorns to tell everyone in attendance that the game had been canceled. Hundreds of disappointed fans who had streamed out of the park waited around just to chat with Hawkins and Brown, and to get autographs from the two schoolboys who were destined for stardom.

That fall, Hawkins accepted a scholarship to Iowa and Brown

received one from Dayton. Both were freshmen at their respective schools in 1961, when college basketball was rocked by a
point-shaving scandal. Jack Molinas, a former Columbia all-
American who was banned for life by the NBA in the 1953–54
season for betting on games while a member of the Fort Wayne
Pistons, was eventually convicted as the mastermind.

Because Hawkins and Brown had known Molinas, and he

Connie "The Hawk" Hawkins during his brief college career
(*New York Times*)

had lent them money, bought them dinner, and let them use his
car, they were implicated in the scandal. Though no evidence
ever surfaced that Brown or Hawkins ever bet on college basketball, both players lost their college scholarships and never
played a varsity game for their respective universities.

In turn, both players were effectively blacklisted by the NBA. "I went into a shell," Brown told William C. Rhoden of the *New York Times* in February 1997, just one month before he died of liver cancer. "I became an introvert. The fact that here you had a life, and you had a future. Now it's gone, taken away from you."

After the banishment, Hawkins went on to play for the Pittsburgh Rens of the American Basketball League (as its nineteen-year-old most valuable player), and also played for the Harlem Globetrotters. Brown took a job as the night-shift operator at the General Motors plant in Dayton, Ohio.

When the American Basketball Association (ABA) was formed in 1967, both players finally had their chance to play professionally. Hawkins joined the Pittsburgh Pipers, winning the league's first most valuable player award in 1968 before going to court and winning the right to play for an NBA team. In 1969 he joined the Phoenix Suns, where he played for four seasons, and still serves the organization as its community relations representative. Brown signed up with the Indiana Pacers in 1967.

Before the ABA and NBA merged in 1976, several ABA players had jumped to established NBA teams, but Brown decided to stay with Indiana as a way of thanking the organization for giving him another chance.

In his eight seasons with the Pacers, Brown averaged 17.4 points per game, winning three championships and playing for the title five times.

Another Rucker star in those days was a teammate of Hawkins at Boys High named Billy Burwell, a fellow Brooklynite who electrified high school crowds at the old Madison Square Garden on 50th Street and Eighth Avenue by dunking two balls in succession through the basket, one powerful slam from his left hand followed by a rim-rocking flush with his right, the balls appearing in his massive mitts like a couple of oranges. Always choreographed to the trumpeting tunes of the Boys High band, Burwell's pregame feat had opponents psychologically defeated even before the opening tip.

At Rucker Park, Burwell sent tremors through the asphalt with the same kind of intimidating dunks. The spectacular air show left many a Rucker faithful who had never seen Burwell dazed and confused. This was the same player they had seen only moments before, shuffling his feet as he entered the park wearing his trademark farmer's overalls. But everyone soon learned that when Billy Burwell shed the country image, he played a city game as big as Manhattan itself.

With all these big-time players arriving to play in his tournament, Holcombe Rucker began asking Parks Department officials for a new and bigger site to stage his games, but still, he did not get much cooperation.

"I remember Holcombe always talking about this female supervisor giving him a hard time about everything he asked for," said Emie Morris. "All the guy ever wanted to do was provide the best possible atmosphere for us kids to play in. When the Parks Department didn't help him out, Holcombe was smart enough to make do with what he had. He was a very resourceful guy."

"The Moment"

As big as Billy Burwell's game was in the early 1960s, Jackie Jackson's was even bigger. Just ask Bruce Spraggins and Cal Ramsey, both of whom consider "The Moment" their fondest Rucker memory.

It is a moment that belongs to Jumping Jackie Jackson. It also belongs to a few dozen aging basketball players and several thousand witnesses who have been playing that one sequence over and over again in their minds for the better part of forty years. The greatest twenty seconds in the history of hoops, according to those who lived it, took place in the summer of 1962, early in the second half of a Rucker Pro game between Big Wilt's Small's

Wilt Chamberlain's back (Big Wilt's Small's Paradise) *(Cal Ramsey)*

Paradise, anchored by you-know-who, and the Brooklyn All-Stars, led by Jumping Jackie.

Chamberlain, the Shaquille O'Neal of his generation who was playing with Philadelphia of the NBA at that time, was the natural center of attention on Big Wilt's Small's Paradise, the team named after the popular Harlem nightclub that Chamberlain now owned, the same nightclub where Holcombe Rucker had met his wife Mary years before.

Big Wilt's Small's Paradise, the team, would have been a legitimate contender for an NBA crown in any decade. Twinkling alongside the Big Dipper were Cal Ramsey and Satch Sanders at the forward spots, and the backcourt featured Russell Cunningham, who had teamed with Ramsey at Commerce High School and at NYU, and the late, great Clinton Roberts, a New York kid who was sent by Holcombe Rucker to Laurinburg Institute in North Carolina before moving on to Winston-Salem Teachers College. Laurinburg was the same place where the Pied Piper sent players like Ernie Morris and Earl Manigault, and future pros like Charlie Scott and Jimmy Walker.

The first man off of Big Wilt's deep bench was Wally Choice, a six five all-American at Indiana. The roster also included Roger Gibbs, the six three guard from Virginia Union; Ralph "Durango Kid" Bacote; Alfred Barden of Boys High, who was best known for holding the high-scoring Tony Jackson to just 13 points in the Boys High championship game victory over Thomas Jefferson in 1957; and Walter Simon, a six six forward who played with New Jersey and Kentucky of the ABA. The coach was a small man in tall standing named Elverald "Shrimp" Walsh, who got the coaching gig because he was a friend of Chamberlain's and because he simply was not good enough to play in the league.

"We had the best team that's ever been out there," said Gibbs, now an accountant living in Harlem. "It's not even worth arguing about."

The Brooklyn squad was a powerhouse in its own right.

Walt Bellamy, the same man who would be brought to New York years later as the Knicks' answer to Chamberlain and Boston's Bill Russell, was Brooklyn's tower of power at center. A collegiate star at Indiana, the six eleven Bellamy was playing professionally at that time with the Chicago Bulls. Joining Bells along Brooklyn's front line were the Hawk, Connie Hawkins, and the Prom Boy, Bruce Spraggins. The explosive backcourt was fueled by Jumping Jackie and the Czar himself, Eddie Simmons.

"No player Connie Hawkins's size could do the things the Hawk could do with a basketball back then," Spraggins said. Then the Prom Boy came gushing out of him again. "Man, both those teams were so awesome," he said. "I'll never forget the crowds, and all the people hanging from everywhere. It was the best time of my life."

The players who remember most say that this championship game between Big Wilt's and the Brooklyn All-Stars was still a close one in the early moments of the second half. That's when Jumping Jackie stepped onto the world's largest basketball stage, and in a mere twenty seconds earned his ticket to immortality.

With Big Wilt's team in possession of the basketball, the rock went down low to the big fella, who spun and flicked up one of his patented finger rolls. At seven one, Chamberlain's shot did not have far to travel when it left his huge digits. Yet, while the ball was still traveling skyward, Jumping Jackie hit the runway. The mighty springs in his legs took him eye-level with Chamberlain's shot, and as the huge crowd stared in disbelief, Jumping Jackie pinned Wilt's shot on the board, angering and embarrassing the Big Dipper. But the show was only just beginning.

Jumping Jackie pitched the ball to the Hawk, and he and Wilt became a blur in offensive transition. When both players reappeared in the middle of the court, Hawkins drilled a pass into Jumping Jackie's breadbasket. Wilt stayed hot on Jumping Jackie's trail, eager to return the rejection notice.

Jumping Jackie dribbled left and began another takeoff just inside the foul line as Wilt backpedaled, timing his return-to-sender swat the whole while.

And then it happened: Jumping Jackie went airborne, holding the ball high over his head with two hands as he began his descent back down on the rim. As he looked down, Jumping Jackie realized that Wilt had beat him to the spot defensively beneath the basket, and now Goliath was waiting to swallow David's shot before a large, screaming crowd that expected nothing less.

"I had no choice," Jackson recalled. "I had to keep going."

And he did. Just before Chamberlain's huge mitt could snuff out the shot, Jumping Jackie pulled it back down and, still gliding in midair, went past Chamberlain, floated to the other side of the basket like a butterfly in tank top and shorts, and in one final, otherworldly twist, his back now facing the basket, stretched out every inch of his six five frame and assaulted the rim with a vicious reverse jam that shook spectators out of the trees and onto the court. It forced the game to be held up for nearly twenty minutes as Jumping Jackie gave high-fives all around. The people who were there that day just wanted to touch Jumping Jackie, to make sure he was really human.

"Hundreds of people just ran out on the court. It was wild," Jackson said of that day. "But the whole thing got Wilt real mad."

Jumping Jackie Jackson in his Globetrotter days *(Jackie Jackson)*

Indeed, Jumping Jackie and his Brooklyn pals had earned the wrath of Chamberlain. The next time down the floor, Chamberlain demanded the ball, and with Bellamy draped all over him, the Big Dipper rose like a tidal wave toward the basket, tossing Bellamy to the asphalt like a rag doll before dropping a thunderous dunk through the cords that seemed to tilt one side of the park in Big Wilt's direction.

"Wilt got so mad," Gibbs said. "All I can remember is seeing his armpits and head way above the rim, just ramming the ball through the basket."

Wilt's next four trips down the floor, all dunks, were just as humiliating for Bellamy, who watched the Big Dipper do his thing from the seat of his pants.

"Connie came over to me and said, 'Oh God, Jackie, why did you have to get the big fella so mad, he's killing poor Walt,' " Jackson said.

The wrath of Chamberlain was also being felt on the big chalk scoreboard as the game soon became a lopsided affair, with Wilt and company winning easily.

"As great as we were, we never beat those guys," Jackson said. "But we gave them games they'll remember forever and a day."

To the best of memories on both teams, Jumping Jackie's dismissal of Wilt's finger roll was the first of two marquee rejections Chamberlain had to deal with during his Rucker playground reign.

" The one other play that stands out in my mind from all those games against Connie and those Brooklyn kids is the day Connie came to the game late in front of a packed house," recalls Ramsey. "Wilt was dominating as usual."

Then the Hawk swooped in.

"When Connie got into the game, Wilt was being guarded by Bellamy," Ramsey said. "Wilt tried one of his patented turnaround bank shots, and when the ball went up, Connie flew skyward and pinned it right on the glass.

" That stunned Wilt," said Ramsey, "and brought the house down."

Dirty-Hand Joe

There were no games being played on a winter day in 1963, when a January snow blanketed Harlem.

Donald Adams, a teacher and basketball coach at the now-defunct Cooper Junior High School on 120th Street and Madison Avenue, sat behind his desk on one of those frigid early mornings watching his students take an exam. The soft sounds of pencils scratching paper and a few squeaky erasers were all that filled the air, until scraping sounds from the schoolyard two stories below began separating chins from palms throughout the classroom.

Scrape . . . scrape . . . scrape . . .

Adams looked up, told everyone to get back to work, and went to investigate.

"I looked out the window, and there he was again," said Adams, "shoveling snow off the basketball court."

At the tender age of thirteen, young Joe Hammond was already out of school, having dropped out for good as a seventh-grader the year before. Just a youngster when his mother died, his father busy trying to make ends meet, Joe went to live with his grandmother. He slept there on most nights, sleeping in hallways on others, spending all of his time drifting from basketball court to basketball court in search of a game. Nothing mattered, not the season or the weather, or even the time of day. Blisters on his fingers, duct tape holding his Pro Keds together, he shot baskets from sunup till long past sundown. And on those days when Mother Nature beat him to the court, Joe Hammond chased her with a shovel or a push broom.

"He spent all of twenty-seven days in the seventh grade," said Howie Evans, sports editor of the *Amsterdam News*. Evans was a basketball director and coach at Harlem's Wagner Center in those years who would become a father figure and mentor to the boy who would one day become known as The Destroyer.

"Joe was a young man, virtually homeless," Evans said. "At the age of eleven and twelve he got real serious about playing basketball, and he would just wander around the parks or the indoor gyms and just shoot and shoot for hours at a time. By watching the older guys play and constantly practicing, he taught himself a lot of different basketball skills.

"By the time he was thirteen, Joe's knowledge of the game was uncanny, and as a guy who had coached thousands of kids before him, I had never seen anyone Joe's age doing the things on a basketball court that he was doing," Evans said. "He was a superb ball handler, and he soon began dominating kids his own age. It's rare to see a young man orchestrate the other four players on the court when the ball is not in his hands, but that's what Joe would do. And very often he'd get frustrated and yell at kids on the court who didn't make the right pass or the right cut, and I'd have to pull him aside and explain to him that those kids were not as developed basketballwise as he was."

Evans and other members of the community took turns taking young Hammond into their homes, feeding and clothing him, a kindness that Hammond would never forget, and would one day repay.

Eventually Hammond found a way to support himself. After playing ball every night, he'd often stumble upon two or three games of craps being played by hustlers beneath the streetlights in his neighborhood. One night he stopped his dribble, and through hazy streams of cigarette and cigar smoke watched the older men shoot dice.

"Then one day a guy was on a roll, and he handed me the dice and said, 'C'mon kid, roll me a winner,'" Hammond said. "Before long, I was hooked."

Soon Hammond was making enough money rolling sevens and hitting the point to pay his grandmother's rent.

"You could jump in a game with fifty dollars, get hot, and work your way into the thousands," he said. "It happened to me plenty of times."

With all his time split now between basketball and dice, Hammond's hands were filthy-black from both street games by the end of every day. That's how he got his first nickname: Dirty-Hand Joe.

By the time he was sixteen, Dirty-Hand Joe was playing hoops against and outshining college and professional players at the Rucker Tournament and in hoop leagues around the city. He began winning championships and MVP awards by ringing up 50- and 60-point games with and against players like Cazzie Russell, Dave Stallworth, and Connie Hawkins.

"I remember my trophy room at my grandmother's house," Hammond said. "I had hundreds of trophies in there, some eight feet tall. Everyone who walked in there just called it the Joe Hammond Museum."

In that same room, Hammond began hiding the several thousand dollars he had earned playing craps, some of that money stuffed in sweat socks and pillowcases, beneath his mattress, and between the pages of unread schoolbooks. He had by now gained a reputation as a master crapsman, and high rollers from Harlem and other parts of New York City were now challenging him to their own games of one-on-one. In either sport, it seemed, Hammond couldn't lose.

Dirty-Hand Joe would soon begin thinking of ways to invest that money. In the meantime, he kept doing the two things he loved more than anything else, and he kept doing them better than anyone else.

Leaving a Legacy

By 1965, the last year of Rucker's life, he got his wish to move his tournament to a prime location. The Parks Department had finally relented, transferring Rucker from the park he had supervised on 130th Street and Seventh Avenue to a park on 151st Street and Harlem River Drive, and then to 155th Street and Eighth Avenue, across from what was now the Polo Grounds projects.

"He was no longer in charge of recreation at 130th Street," said Ernie Morris. "So when he got transferred, he took his tournament with him."

The last park, the one on 155th Street that bears his name, became in effect Harlem's town square, that special place where on magical summer evenings some of the world's greatest athletes performed on a unique stage. And when the rock wasn't bouncing at Holcombe's place, friends would still meet up at Rucker Park just to chat, local businessmen to recruit workers, and community leaders and activists to educate neighborhood folk about the civil rights movement.

Seventeen summers after tossing up the first jump ball on an outdoor court, Rucker's tournament stood as tall and proud as Wilt The Stilt himself. There were no corporate sponsors hanging banners on the fences around the court, but the people, especially those people who loved watching big-time baskets, already held Rucker's showcase in the same reverence as they did the monster games of The Hawk and Roger Brown.

And the players themselves, especially the pros, suddenly found that they needed Holcombe Rucker more than he needed them.

"I got more exposure playing in the Rucker Tournament than I did in my four years at Virginia Union," said Spraggins, who later played with the New York Nets of the ABA in the 1967–68 season.

After one summer in the Rucker Tournament, Spraggins had polished his skills and picked up enough court savvy to make the Eastern Pro League—a precursor to the Continental Basketball Association—with Wilkes-Barre, later becoming one of the first players to sign a contract with the league that used a red, white, and blue ball.

"There's absolutely no question that playing against that kind of high-caliber competition at Rucker improved your game," Cal Ramsey said. "Playing at places like Rucker Park and at other schoolyards around the city against older and tougher competition taught me more about rebounding than I learned from any coach, anywhere."

In March 1965, at the age of thirty-eight, Holcombe Rucker died of lung cancer in a Bronx hospital, not far from where he lived at 1020 East 222nd Street. He left behind Mary and their three children, Phillip, Dennis, and Ramona.

"As great a man as Holcombe was, he did have one vice," said Morris. "He was a chain-smoker, and I mean he smoked profusely."

Rucker died on a Saturday at the Kingsbridge Veterans Hospital in the Bronx and was buried in Long Island's National Cemetery. His wake at the Unity Funeral Home on Eighth Avenue brought long lines of family and friends, including professional athletes as well as doctors, lawyers, educators, businessmen, and schoolteachers who had been steered along their career paths by the Pied Piper. In his heyday, Rucker had used his vast network of contacts from around the country to help enroll many of them in college. And now they were back to thank the man for all he had done in making their world a better place, and to tell him one last time how much they loved him.

"It's amazing, my husband had a great influence on all these people, a greater influence on them than their own parents had," Mary Rucker said. "He was a wonderful person, he really was. He always believed in who he was and what he was doing. You know, it's not easy to find someone in life who is really and truly interested in what you're all about."

Just days after Rucker's untimely death, Howie Evans wrote what many Harlemites were feeling as they grieved a friend who left them years too soon.

"Yes, Holcombe Rucker was burdened with the weight of Harlem, a Harlem so heavy with frustration that all of your Adam Powells, James Farmers, Malcolm X's, etc., had barely gotten it off the ground. Yet somehow, you can say Holcombe Rucker did as much or even more than all the others combined in his one-man crusade to bring Harlem an image of respectability and decency.

"What Holcombe Rucker has begun must not be interrupted," the column continued. "The foundation is solid, the die has been cast. It remains for us to continue so that all that has taken place will not have been in vain. No finer tribute could be given to Holcombe, than the one of knowing his baby tournament, 'Rucker's,' is growing bigger and better every summer."

The park at 155th Street, Rucker's last site and the place where ballers from every corner of the basketball universe still bring their duffel bags and fancy games, was officially dedicated in his name by Mayor John V. Lindsay on July 13, 1969. One year later, on July 26, 1970, the entire area around Rucker Park was designated Holcombe Rucker Square via proclamation by the Honorable Percy Sutton, then the Manhattan borough president.

"For all he did for his community and summer basketball in general, Holcombe deserved that type of tribute," said Bob Mc-Cullough, a Rucker disciple and former collegiate hoop star out of Benedict College in South Carolina who became the fabled league's commissioner shortly after his mentor's death.

"We're talking about a man who knew that people in the neighborhood couldn't afford to buy tickets to Madison Square Garden to see professional basketball games," said McCullough, who was drafted by the Cincinnati Royals in 1965 (he was the nation's second leading collegiate scorer that season behind Rick Barry), but was released when another star guard, Oscar Robertson, ended his holdout.

"So therefore, in essence," said McCullough, "Holcombe Rucker brought Madison Square Garden to the kids in New York's inner city by having the pros play in his tournament."

By the time he passed away, Holcombe Rucker had done a lot more than that. Having run tournaments largely out of his own pockets for seventeen years, it was estimated that over 700 disadvantaged youngsters had been helped, tutored, coached, and sent to college by the man, and over 150 professional and semi-pro players owed their careers to him.

"I was just a kid when I met him," said Donnie Walsh, current president of the Indiana Pacers. "At the time, I thought Holcombe Rucker was just a guy who ran tournaments in a park, but years later I realized he was far more than that. Sometimes, when you're in the presence of great men, you don't always know it."

Walsh was a white, skinny, and ultratalented all-city guard from Riverdale who starred at Fordham Prep before moving on to North Carolina in 1961 and teaming there in the backcourt with a player named Larry Brown and a first-year head coach named Dean Smith. One day in the summer of 1957 he met face-to-face with the Pied Piper. Walsh, his playing sneakers wrapped around his neck just in case a game broke out, had been sent to the park by a scout named Harry Gotkin, who told him he could find top-notch competition there. Walsh was a recognized name throughout the five boroughs, having been chosen by a coach named Mike Tynberg to play for his team, the Gems, which brought together the city's best schoolboy stars.

"I didn't have my own team or anything," Walsh said. "I met Mr. Rucker at the park and he put me on one of his college teams. Holcombe was a very well-spoken guy, very gentle in his demeanor—he had no agenda."

The very next Sunday, Walsh, who had never been to Harlem, was back in the park again, playing sneakers still wrapped around his neck. Though basketball has taken him to many places since, the atmosphere on that one afternoon still sends chills up his spine.

"There must have been over one thousand people in that little, fenced-in schoolyard," Walsh said. "There is really no way to capture the feeling of what it was like playing up there, with all those great players, and it didn't matter if you were black or white, because if you showed the crowd you were a player, they respected you for it. I was a good player, but I had never played in front of so many people before."

Admittedly nervous at first, Walsh soon thrilled the crowd with his fancy ballhandling. "This guy was a bad mother," said Morris, referring to Walsh's behind-the-back dribbling and no-look passes. "I mean, he was the Abdullah-Mullah-Dullah of his day."

Walsh said he received more thrills than he ever gave to the raucous Rucker crowds. "It was one of the best parts of my young life," he said. "As far as basketball goes, I have never, ever had such a great feeling about being a part of the game, and I've been to the NBA finals with the Pacers.

"I guess the only thing I can relate it to," said Walsh, "would be older guys who love music telling me about the thrills of playing in jam sessions with great musicians of the thirties and forties. That's the kind of feeling you had playing up there."

In the summer months that followed Rucker's death, Bob McCullough, former New York Knick Freddie Crawford, Arlington "Ollie" Edinboro, Ernie Morris, Ed Warner, and others worked to keep Rucker's dream alive. Calling themselves the Holcombe Rucker Memorial Committee, they sent hundreds of Harlem hoopsters to college on scholarships, the money received from local banks and the city government.

The Memorial Committee's headquarters was located at I.S. 201, a grammar school on 127th Street between Park and Madison Avenues. In the same building, Rucker's followers ran the Each-One-Teach-One Center. Named for their mentor's favorite motto, Each-One-Teach-One provided basketball and a number of other activities for neighborhood kids as an alternative to wasting their time on the streets. Program directors often invited professional basketball players, doctors, lawyers, and schoolteachers to talk with the kids about the importance of staying in school and achieving their goals.

By 1966, however, the Memorial Committee had split into two factions. Bob McCullough ran the pro division of the Rucker Tournament, which would change its name to the Harlem Professional Basketball League by 1971. Other members operated the high school and college divisions, which were now independent of the pro league. The split got nasty at times, with both sides often fighting for financial contributions from the same sponsors. With eighty-seven teams and thousands of youngsters from Harlem and other parts of New York City participating, the Rucker Community League, which ran the high school and college divisions, had to stage a number of games at Mount Morris Park on 121st Street and Madison Avenue (now called Marcus Garvey Park), and at the Colonel Young Playground on 145th Street and Lenox Avenue.

Despite the formation of the Harlem Professional Basketball League, most of the seven thousand people who flocked to tiny Rucker Park every weekend to watch the five games put on by the league still called it the Rucker Tournament.

"The confusion about the difference is somewhat akin to New Yorkers' insistence on calling the Avenue of the Americas 'Sixth Avenue,' " Al Harvin of the *New York Times* wrote in an article about the tournament published July 4, 1971.

The Rivalry Continues

By the middle of the 1960s, the New York–Philadelphia rivalry was in full swing at Rucker Park, as Philly players traveled by train, bus, car, and thumb to get to the annual clash. These were the only games in which Wilt Chamberlain did not play with his New York buddies, opting instead to team with his true homeboys, the kids he grew up competing with and against in the City of Brotherly Love.

"We were a team made up mostly of jump-shooters, and New York had more of a give-and-go type team," said Jay Norman, the Temple star who played in the Eastern League before becoming an assistant basketball coach with the Owls from 1968 to 1989. "Very often, Wilt was out of basketball shape when we played those games, so we tried to get the New York guys to take him back for a day," Norman half-joked. "Don't get me wrong now, when Wilt really felt like playing, he would just shut down the basket on anyone, period."

Rolling along the sidelines at Holcombe Rucker's tournament in the mid-1960s was the Philadelphia coach, Victor Harris, a young man who had been stricken by polio when he was eighteen and was now confined to a wheelchair. "Victor was a very intelligent person and a good coach," Norman said. "The guys didn't mind playing for him."

Harris had been a fine basketball player in his own right at West Philadelphia High School—where future pros Ray "Chink" Scott and Gene Banks also played—before the disease found him. He was the man mostly responsible for putting together the Philly squad, which also included longtime Temple coach Don Chaney, Sonny Lloyd of Maryland State, Dave Riddick of the University of Maryland–Eastern Shore, and Sonny Hill of Central State University (Ohio), who enjoyed a ten-year career in the Eastern League.

"The games against New York were very competitive because reputations were at stake," said Hill, sixty-six, who is now executive adviser to the Philadelphia 76ers. "A reputation could be made, or broken," he said, "on a single play."

While the large and raucous Rucker crowds could get butterflies fluttering even in the stomachs of their hometown heroes, the Philly crew was already used to playing in such an intense atmosphere, having wowed standing-room-only crowds in Philly's famous Baker League and at outdoor parks like Moylan Recreation Center (now called Hank Gathers Park) on 25th and Diamond, and Haddington Recreation Center (now called Wilt Chamberlain Park) on 57th and Haverford.

"On both sides, it was a *Who's Who* list of players competing," Hill said. "And the players from each side had the highest amount of respect for one another. It was the golden age, a time when both cities were major contributors to basketball in this country. It was a time when the level of competition was at its highest peak."

While no one player from either side of the Hudson River will go on record saying which city won more games during that golden era, Hill did offer a shared mind-set: "Historically, the wins and losses have probably been fifty-fifty," Hill said, "but when we tell our lies throughout the years, New York won more than Philly did, and Philly more than New York."

Hill, a five ten guard who first made a name for himself at Northeast High School, went on to found the Baker League as well as the talent-laden Sonny Hill League, which has helped produce more than a dozen current NBA stars including Kobe Bryant, Rasheed Wallace, Aaron McKie, and Malik Rose.

Having served his city honorably in hoop battle for fourteen years from 1955 through 1969, Hill remains the only player from the great New York–Philly rivalry to win the MVP award twice, a phenomenal achievement considering the names that filled both rosters during that period of time.

"Those games were as big as NBA championship games," Hill said. "Those games were about pride, and if you were a great player of any essence from one of those two cities, you played in those games."

And as surely as the Rucker League had its share of lesser-known but equally talented hoop stars, so too did the Baker League. Philly would often bring to New York its secret weapon, a not-so-poor-man's Rodgers and Lear named Tee Parham, an explosive five ten guard who didn't have the grades to get into Temple, but scored straight A's against some of the top schoolyard competition in the universe.

"This was one bad player," Ernie Morris said. "I mean, this kid used to kill guys on the court for the love of killing. Back in the day, he was on the order of a Guy Rodgers and the King himself. In fact, a couple of longtime pros named Walt Hazzard and Wali Jones were like caddies to this guy."

Jay Norman remembers New York's biggest stars being Cal Ramsey and Satch Sanders. His mind racing back to all those great players and the intense rivalry between the two cities, Norman remembered the time when the New York crew embarrassed Philly's not-so-gentle giant in front of a packed Rucker mob. "Wilt got so mad that one time he dunked the ball with all of his might, and the basket was vibrating for close to five minutes. Everyone just stopped what they were doing and watched that basket rattle and rattle. It was quite a scene."

Black Jesus Comes to Harlem

Another great scene from the New York–Philadelphia rivalry took place in the summer of 1966, when Tony Greer crossed basketball paths with Philly's Earl "The Pearl" Monroe.

"Yes, that was my fifteen minutes of fame," said Greer. "That's the day I went head-to-head with Black Jesus."

Greer, a six three all-American center who was voted Catholic high school player of the year at St. Francis Prep High School in 1960, was referring to a classic matchup between the two cities held in New York, this one at Mount Morris Park the summer after Holcombe Rucker passed away.

One of the first black players recruited by St. Francis Prep, Greer had played his college ball at St. Anselm's in Manchester, New Hampshire, coached there by a former NYU star named Al Grenert, a white player who barnstormed in the 1940s with great black teams that included William "Pop" Gates and John Isaacs.

At St. Anselm's, a lily-white college in a lily-white New England community, Greer had felt his share of racial tension, though he had not known the kind of antiblack sentiment that Rucker kids like Jumping Jackie Jackson and Richard "Skinny" Reed experienced while attending colleges in the South.

Greer roomed with Myles Dorch, a Bronx kid and Rucker alum who had starred at Cardinal Hayes High School and was a member of the Hayes squad that eliminated Greer and the St. Francis crew from the Catholic High School Athletic Association (CHSAA) playoffs in 1960. He remembers what life was like when the two walked into a restaurant, or a library, or any other public place where whites had gathered.

"You remember that great E. F. Hutton commercial, where everyone is carrying on and making noise until E. F. Hutton speaks, and then the place gets real quiet?" asks Greer. "Well, that's how it was when Myles and I went into one of these places—white folks would just stop what they were doing and stare at us, as if we were from outer space or something."

And that's precisely the kind of look left on the face of Earl "The Pearl" Monroe, a spinning, stutter-stepping, ballhandling wizard and scoring machine from Winston-Salem State otherwise known as Black Jesus, after his brilliant basketball path crossed through Tony Greer's neighborhood.

Monroe began hearing people refer to him as "Pearl" during the 1967 season at Winston-Salem, when his scoring totals of 38, 68, 58, 53, and 55 points over five games that season ran in a local paper under the headline "THESE ARE EARL'S PEARLS." Since he was a teenager on the Philly playgrounds, people first began calling him Black Jesus as a tribute to the miracles he performed on the blacktop.

On that day at Mount Morris Park in 1966, a large Philadelphia contingent made up mostly of Black Jesus disciples had arrived to root for Monroe and superskilled teammates like Teddy Campbell, a six six bruiser from North Carolina A&T State University who intimidated opposing players on the hardwood as well as the asphalt.

Greer was a borderline selection to play in the annual classic. Howie Evans, the New York coach, did not feel that Greer was up to the challenge of handling Black Jesus and was looking for a bigger-name guard until Ernie Morris convinced Evans that Greer was their man. He was joined in the backcourt by a young Harlemite and speed demon from Norfolk State named Richard "Pee Wee" Kirkland, whom *Sports Illustrated* was calling "maybe the fastest man in college basketball."

Up front for New York was a sensational six four forward named Bobby Hunter, who had starred at Seward Park High School and would later hook up with the Harlem Globetrotters, as well as a high-scoring Harlem phenom named Rodney Butler, a six two swingman who played at George Washington High School before moving on to Western New England College. Butler never played pro ball, but in the pro division of Holcombe Rucker's showcase, he was dropping 40 points per game on anyone who dared guard him.

Despite New York's talented threesome, the team did not have a player beefy and talented enough to match the size and strength of Campbell, who was licking his chops and clapping his shot-blocking hands on the layup line minutes before the opening tip.

Realizing they were about to lose the frontline battle to their Philly counterparts, Evans, Morris, and the rest of the Big Apple bunch looked up into the stands and found a tall, skinny kid named Lew Alcindor sitting there.

Alcindor, who had led mighty Power Memorial High School to three straight CHSAA titles from 1963 to 1965, and had just led John Wooden's UCLA Bruins to the first of three straight NCAA championships, had not yet changed his name to Kareem Abdul-Jabbar, and his body had not yet grown to its full seven feet two inches in height.

"Yo, Lew, you got your sneakers on?" Morris shouted.

"Uh, yeah?" said a startled Alcindor, who had simply come to the game as a spectator.

"Well, get your skinny ass down here!" Morris shouted.

Which he did, and while Alcindor was shutting down Campbell—Philadelphia did not protest the move—Black Jesus and Tony Greer were waging unholy hoop war.

"Monroe did not know I could shoot or play defense," said Greer, "but in college, I had always guarded the other team's top scorer, and I was a pretty decent scorer myself.

"Before the game, Earl stared me down, and with a blank expression on his face, said to his teammates, 'I got him.' "

Greer, perhaps the only player in the city at that time playing with a shaved head, looked a lot more menacing to Black Jesus when the game began. With something to prove to Evans, his parents watching from the bleachers, the more than a thousand fans from both cities in attendance, and most important, himself, Greer preached his own brand of basketball to Black Jesus, firing away from all angles and giving the Pearl a twisting, spinning, cross-overing dose of his own medicine en route to a 30-point explosion and the most valuable player trophy.

Long before New York defeated Philadelphia in that game, Black Jesus, dazed and confused, had fouled out chasing the determined Greer all over the court.

"Apparently, Earl was used to playing against guards who couldn't move as well or maneuver on the court like I could," Greer said. "I'm pretty sure he still remembers my name."

Several years later, Earl The Pearl was back in Harlem, having a drink at Big Wilt's Small's Paradise, when he called over a man named Charlie Polk, who was the emcee at Big Wilt's.

"Hey," The Pearl asked Polk, "whatever happened to that Tony Greer dude?" He hadn't forgotten.

Though he never played pro ball, Greer became a parole officer and social worker. Officially retired from those jobs at the age of sixty, Greer is now the women's basketball coach at Wings Academy High School in the Bronx. Greer still lives in Harlem and is still stopped on the street almost daily and asked to retell the tale of his encounter with Black Jesus.

"I meet guys all the time who want to talk about it," said Greer, a Rucker Park Hall of Famer. "Everybody I've talked to over the years claims to have been in the park that day, but there aren't that many seats in Madison Square Garden."

Clyde and the Copter

One young, dynamic player who filled those Madison Square
Garden seats in the glory days of the New York Knicks was Walt
"Clyde" Frazier, whose playground career lasted all of one very
long day. . . .

Sprinting up and down the Rucker court, Archie Clark
needed a breather, so coach Carl Green called a time-out and
huddled his crew together along the sidelines. Green was attempting to nurse a slim lead in the second half of the 1969
Rucker Championship contest between his Rucker Pros and a
top-flight playground squad called the Colonial All-Stars.

The Rucker Pros featured Frazier and two other Knicks,
Willis Reed and Freddie Crawford, along with Bob McCullough,
Chink Scott, Howie Komives, Pee Wee Kirkland, and Bruce
Spraggins.

The Colonial All-Stars were propelled by a skywalking asphalt
god named Herman "Helicopter" Knowings. The Colonial All-
Stars, which also featured the great Willie Hall, were defending
league champions, having turned aside a Rucker Pros squad that
included Reed, Bill Bradley, Mike Riordan, and an assortment of
other New York Knicks the previous summer.

"Helicopter Knowings was quite a player," said Jay Norman,
the Philadelphia star who tangled with the Copter on several
occasions. "But like many of those great New York leapers, if
you gave him a pretty good bump before takeoff, he had a
pretty turbulent flight and didn't always come down with the
ball. Hey, I was a guy who had to make a living holding down
guys five and six inches taller than me. I had to do what I had
to do."

During the time-out that day, Green called on the services of the young Knick whom Willis Reed had brought to the park for a single day, just to help out in crunch time.

Frazier, the flashy six-foot-four-inch guard out of Southern Illinois who had already won over the Madison Square Garden faithful with an exhilarating game that earned him a spot on the NBA's All-Rookie Team, leaped off the bench and into the heat of Holcombe Rucker's sizzling summer finale. He was greeted by thousands of screaming fans whose booming cheers, cleverly orchestrated chants, and constant chiding made it nearly impossible to hear the bounce of the basketball from the folding chairs at courtside, where bench players from both teams sat and watched.

As Frazier took the ball upcourt for the Rucker Pros, the noise that filled the park reached an intimidating crescendo, as most spectators had been rooting since the opening tip for the Copter and company to pull off another upset.

"It was like being in the Old West and running into all those gunslingers," said Frazier, who now does color commentary on Knick broadcasts. "Guys were dunking the ball all over the place, it was wild. Everybody was after me that day because I was the Knicks' number one draft choice, so they all were trying to show me up."

With the jaws of the crowd clamping down harder on his every move, with its collective digs cutting deeper and deeper beneath Clyde's thin skin as the minutes wore on, something unusual, and even unthinkable, happened to the great Walt Frazier, the consummate captain of cool. In the eye of the storm, for maybe the only time in his whole career, he was blown off his mighty game.

"He got nervous," Green recalled. "The park was just so packed that day; it shook him up.

"Even though he had played before NBA crowds all across the country," said Green, "he just wasn't used to this kind of commotion. I mean, people were just hollering at the poor guy."

Green struggled with the decision to pull Frazier from the game. Should he protect his lead, or should he protect the ego of his young superstar?

"He just wasn't playing well, so I decided to take him out," said Green, whose Rucker Pros would go on to win their second championship in a three-year span. "He got so mad at me when I pulled him and stayed mad at me for a long time, but me and him are cool now."

Years after Clyde The Glide had led the Knicks to a pair of world championships, he jumped back into a defensive posture when I mentioned some of those Rucker playground stars in the same breath as his NBA brethren.

"Many of those guys could jump out of the gym but they couldn't dribble or didn't have a perimeter shot," Frazier said. "They were schoolyard legends and guys would always say, 'Oh, they could play in the NBA,' but it was questionable because they had so many glaring weaknesses, and if you put those guys in a pro game, they wouldn't know how to set a pick-and-roll or do backdoor plays or execute the basic fundamentals of the game.

"It was just one-on-one showtime stuff," said one of the NBA's master showmen. "It was kind of like the NBA is today, with guys shaking and baking, with the crowd oooh-ing and aaah-ing, but there was no team structure involved."

Frazier echoes the words of many other pros who left Rucker Park a little red-faced in those years, saying that playground legends usually had an advantage over their professional counter-parts simply because the rules of the game were overlooked in favor of a good show.

"In the parks you could goaltend or you could travel, and nothing would be called," Frazier said. "That's why I didn't like it.

"You also have to realize that for the playground stars, playing against NBA competition was their NBA season. We were just up there playing in the off-season and not as serious as they were. They certainly had more incentive than we had."

Let it be known that Walt Frazier was not the only Knick blushing on the court that historic day at Holcombe Rucker's place.

Willis Reed, the six ten captain of the Knicks who had won the hearts of Garden fans with brilliant battles in the paint against visiting giants like Wilt Chamberlain and Bill Russell, caught a pass ahead of the field early in the first half of the Rucker Championship contest and stormed toward the hoop for what looked like an easy throwdown.

"Except he didn't know the Copter was coming," said Lou Huston, who played alongside Mr. Knowings on the Colonial All-Stars that day.

As Reed crossed the foul line heading in for the rim-rocker, the six five Copter was just crossing the half-court line, putting his engine into a gear even he did not know existed.

"From there, the way the Copter was picking up steam, it looked like Willis was moving in slow motion," Huston said. "He caught Willis's dunk attempt just in the nick of time and swatted it away like a big old fly, and the place went nuts."

Though Copter's crew crash-landed in the end, Herman Knowings left his calling card later that day. On one sequence just before the end of the second half, Copter destroyed the egos of three pros who shall remain nameless, players from both sides insist, so as to keep their reps intact.

"I'm not going to mention names, because they are my friends," said McCullough, "but there was one play where the Pros brought the ball down, and Copter blocked a shot. Whap! The guy passed the ball to a teammate, who tried to shoot. Whap! Blocked again. The next guy passed the ball to a third pro. Whap! Blocked again. You get the picture? Copter blocked three shots in a row by professionals."

Huston summed up what players from both sides, and the thousands of fans who were treated to the basketball wonders of Herman Knowings, are still feeling: "I miss the Copter. We all do, man. That guy, I swear, he used to fly like an angel."

Herman "Helicopter" Knowings was born in South Carolina, but his family moved to Harlem when he was young. He made a name for himself first at the Wagner Center on 120th Street in East Harlem playing in year-round tournaments against the best players the city had to offer, and later at Rucker Park. One day at Rucker, the Copter was hovering above players who were half a foot taller than he. A player named Walter "Rodin" Simpson, who was announcing the game that day, dubbed Herman Knowings the Helicopter Man.

In *The City Game*, written by Pete Axthelm in 1970, Knowings is described as being "among the most remarkable playground phenomena." Axthelm wrote that Knowings, then in his late twenties, was "uneducated and unable to break into pro ball," but added that "the Helicopter has managed to retain the spring in his legs and the willpower to remain at the summit after many of his contemporaries have faded from the basketball scene."

Axthelm also noted that "Knowings can send waves of electricity through a park with his mere presence. . . . when he goes up to block a shot, he seems to hover endlessly in midair above his prey, daring him to shoot—and then blocking whatever shot his hapless foe attempts. Like most memorable playground moves, it is not only effective but magnetic. As Knowings goes up, the crowd shouts, 'Fly, 'copter, fly,' and seems to share his heady trip. When he shoves the ball down the throat of a visiting NBA star—as he often does in the Rucker Tournament—the Helicopter inflates the pride of a whole neighborhood."

The Goat and Lew Alcindor

Herman The Helicopter had followed Jackie Jackson as Rucker Park's highest-flying showman. That long line of premier leapers was continued by Earl Manigault, the man they called Goat.

I first got to meet Manigault on a February morning in 1995. A warm sun had made a surprise appearance and now it was smiling bright on a group of young boys tuning up their jams on the rusted rims at the Happy Warrior Playground in West Harlem.

"Nice dunk," one boy said to another. "But can you Goat it?"

More than thirty years after the legend of Earl "The Goat" Manigault was born in the very park where this jam session was taking place, his basketball descendants were still emulating his style, still trying to soar as high as the man who soared higher than most players his size in the history of New York City.

"Here it goes, yo," said another one of the boys, dribbling the ball hard with both hands as he eyed the rim and readied himself for takeoff. "Here goes the Goat Dunk."

The youngster sped toward the hoop, rose off the blacktop,

and in midair, cocked the rock behind his head. As he swooped in on the tin, he let out a primal scream and threw down a monstrous two-handed, tomahawk dunk—Goat style.

"Not bad," said an older man with a soft voice standing behind me, smiling as he took in the air show. "I couldn't have done it better myself."

Dressed in a navy blue winter coat with its collar raised high, eyes glowing beneath the bill of a matching baseball cap and above the lumpy folds of his white knit scarf, the older man looked like a ghost visiting a basketball seance.

This was no ghost, but Earl Manigault in the flesh, the man whom Kareem Abdul-Jabbar once called "the best basketball player his size in the history of New York City."

Scheduled to meet me for an interview, he had arrived just in time to steal the limelight, just as he always did in the 1960s and 1970s before drugs forced a crash landing to his high-flying, promising career.

"This was one of my stages," said Manigault, his dark eyes sweeping across the playground. "Back then, I had a gift that no one else had. I was a little man, but I could fly with the big men.

"Growing up, Kareem and I were very close," he said. "We both had talent and we both ended up taking separate roads in life. He chose his road, and I chose mine, and I paid for it. I look at these kids, and I think back to the good old days. I think back to me and Kareem playing on this very court, practicing our moves and teaching each other how to get to the basket. It was a long time ago, but I still remember telling Kareem that he would never be respected if he didn't play tough. I think I helped him a little bit and he helped me. We both learned a little something from each other. I really loved that guy."

While Jabbar was paving his road toward the Hall of Fame with his sweeping, signature skyhook that left opponents defenseless, Manigault was setting a course for self-destruction on the same mean streets where he would become a folk hero.

"At that time, there weren't a whole lot of people who could do the things with a basketball that Earl Manigault could do," Jabbar said. "He was so talented, so agile, so quick. He used to make so many innovative moves to the hoop. Basketball was his total means of expression."

Basketball was indeed Manigault's only means of expression, and on most evenings when the Harlem sun faded behind the old tenements and slipped into the Hudson River, there was nowhere left for the Goat to roam except the dimly lit, troubled streets beyond the chain-link fence where people had pressed their noses to watch him fly.

"I could go anywhere and get anything I wanted, including drugs," Manigault said. "I used to go over to the East Side and hang out with the Latin brothers or stay right here with the blacks. Remember, I was the Goat. Everybody knew me. Everybody loved me."

As one of the younger players attempted to dribble past Manigault, the Goat reached in with a quick hand and stole the ball.

"It's hard to believe, but all of a sudden, I'm fifty years old," said Manigault, staring into the basketball as if all of his memories were locked inside of it. "Kareem used to stop by the tournament once in a while, but I haven't seen him in years.

"Life is funny that way," he said. "You never know how people are going to turn out."

The love affair between Manigault and New York City began when the Goat was just a teenager, when word of his remarkable

Earl "The Goat" Manigault (*New York Times*)

leaping ability and thunderous dunks over taller, older opponents spread through Harlem like wildfire.

"I had the fluid air game and the ground game to match," said
Manigault, who was six one, 175 pounds during his prime. "At the
time, no little man had both. There weren't too many little guys
soaring to the hoop and dunking on guys six nine and six ten. I
was a pioneer in that sense. That's why I became so popular."

With an astonishing fifty-inch vertical leap, Manigault wowed
the crowds with his dunking and shot-blocking performances on
his home court, and in Rucker League games at the parks on
130th Street and Seventh Avenue and at 155th Street and
Eighth Avenue.

"I was probably the first player to lead the guards from the ground to the air," Manigault said. "I took them from weak layups to strong dunks."

In his Rucker Park heydey, the Goat—who got that nickname from a junior high school teacher who kept pronouncing his last name "Mani-Goat"—dunked over some of the NBA's most famous domes, including the likes of Kareem Abdul-Jabbar, Connie Hawkins, and Willis Reed.

"We used to do all the things that Michael Jordan and the rest

The young Kareem Abdul-Jabbar *(Future Sports)*

of those guys do today, except they were called different names,"
Manigault said. "The three sixty, we used to call that Around the
World. The tomahawk dunk, well, that was the Goat Dunk. I in-
vented that."

In Harlem poolrooms and barbershops, in bars and social
clubs, people still talk about the time when the Goat dunked a
ball backward thirty-six times in a row to win a sixty-dollar bet,
and, as has been written but also often debated, he would rou-
tinely hustle people who bet against his ability to pick quarters
off the tops of backboards.

Harlem hoop junkies have also credited Manigault with yet
another invention—the Double Dunk, where a player dunks the
ball with one hand, catches it with his other hand as it falls
through the cords, and slams it through the basket again.

While Abdul-Jabbar was making a name for himself as an all-
city hoopster at the now-defunct Power Memorial High School
in Manhattan, Manigault became a star at Benjamin Franklin
High School, a basketball powerhouse in the Public Schools
Athletic League.

"Earl and I would get together on certain Saturday mornings
and play a lot of three-on-three basketball in the park or wherever the real good games were being played," Abdul-Jabbar said.
"Earl was more of a street-player than I was, so he never really
got the same type of mainstream recognition that I got in high
school. But people who really knew the game knew that Earl
could play."

The undisciplined attitude that Manigault acquired on the
mean streets directly affected his basketball career, as he was
kicked out of Benjamin Franklin during his senior year for smok-
ing marijuana, a charge he denied until his death. Raised by his
mother, who made ends meet working as a hotel clerk, the Goat

did not have a strong father figure to lean on when the going got rough, which is why he always sought the advice of Holcombe Rucker.

"Earl didn't have a strong fondness for school, and some of those guys that he was hanging around with were headed for a bad ending," Abdul-Jabbar recalled. "They were into drugs and alcohol and a lot of gangster-type things. I never saw Earl doing any of that stuff, because our relationship was built solely on basketball, but I did know that he hung around with them.

"I didn't have any personal knowledge of what he was doing, but I didn't think he would hang out with them and not understand what they were all about," Jabbar continued. "Despite the crowd he was running with, I still felt that he was too talented not to be a part of somebody's college program."

With the help of Holcombe Rucker, who met with Manigault's mother to help decide where her son should go to school, the Goat went on to Laurinburg Institute, a North Carolina prep school, where he played for one year while earning a high school diploma.

During his high school days, the Goat and a star-studded Franklin cast rocked Rucker Park. Joining Manigault on a team called Young Life were all-Americans Larry Newbold, a six four guard who went on to star at Long Island University; Willie Mangum, a six three glass cleaner and vertical voyager widely considered one of the highest leapers in the PSAL; and Aubrey Matthews, a six eight, high-leaping, trash-talking center who is said to have been the first player to successfully dunk two basketballs at the same time, ending every one of his slams with a cocky backpedal while shouting "The Breeze!"—a reference to how cool a customer he really was.

Perhaps the most memorable Goat moment at Rucker Park

came in the summer of 1967 at the expense of Brooklyn USA and one of its star players, Eldridge Webb. Teaming on the Brooklyn squad with Syracuse-bound Vaughn Harper, Webb was a six four all-American from Boys High whose towering leaps to the basketball heavens drew chants of "Boys High—Mambo—Olé—Olé" and earned him the nickname "Steel Springs."

In the early minutes of the second half of that contest, the high-skying rivals left a dent in the clouds when the Goat got out on a fast break, staring at nothing but asphalt between himself and the basket, Steel Springs the closest player to him but still too far back to catch him.

The crowd rose to their feet in anticipation of yet another stylish breakaway jam by the Goat, but on this day, Earl Manigault had other plans. The Goat took two speedy steps toward the hoop before slamming on the brakes, the crowd noise coming to a screeching halt as well.

Still dribbling, the Goat took a sneaky peek over his shoulder, smiled, and waved Steel Springs over in his direction. Steel Springs obliged him, storming toward the Goat with a fury. The Goat then put it into gear and began steaming down the runway.

Just as the Goat reached the rim, Steel Springs reached the Goat. Both players rose off the blacktop with the Goat palming the ball in his right hand, way below his waist, as he ascended toward Harlem folklore. With his arms stretched way above his head, Steel Springs rose to block the would-be dunk.

With Steel Springs's hands still way above the rim, the Goat put his act into that other gear that separated him from most other players, bringing the rock from way behind him as he elevated, and, looking down at Steel Springs's fingertips, windmilling it through the cords before a disbelieving audience.

"One of the greatest dunks I've ever seen," said Joe Hammond. "You had to see the look on Eldridge's face, man. I mean, he couldn't believe it, and neither could we."

Soon after the Goat enrolled at Laurinburg, recruitment letters from North Carolina, Duke, Indiana, and hundreds of other major college basketball programs were being stuffed into Manigault's mailbox.

But the Goat, who had logged more minutes on the streets than in the classroom, felt that he wouldn't be able to handle the academic work at a prominent college, and after consulting again with Mr. Rucker, chose instead to attend Johnson C. Smith University, a predominantly black school in Charlotte, North Carolina.

That decision backfired, as Manigault continued to struggle in the classroom. He didn't get along with his coach, either, and lasted less than a year at the school.

"The coach didn't want to play me in my first year," Manigault said. "He said to me, 'I want to give the seniors a chance.' I looked at him and said, 'The seniors? Are you kidding me? I'm better than all of them.' But he wasn't kidding, and it came down to either me leaving or the coach changing his mind. Finally, I just got up and left."

Depressed and with no desire to play college basketball, Manigault went back to the comforts of his old playground, and to the dangers of his old neighborhood. His schoolyard buddy Kareem was long gone for the West Coast, where he was quickly becoming a household name at UCLA.

"That's when I went right to the bottom," Manigault said. "That's when I started messing with the 'white lady.' "

The "white lady" that Manigault was referring to was heroin.

He became a hard-core junkie, and in order to support his hundred-dollar-per-day addiction, he resorted to thievery. He went as far as stealing mink coats in Manhattan's garment district to support his habit.

A neighborhood legend with NBA potential, an idol to countless thousands who had cheered wildly for him when he performed some of basketball's most remarkable and daring aerial feats, the Goat was now nodding out pathetically in full view of the neighborhood, stumbling to the earth instead of gliding over it.

"It was a real waste, it was tragic," Jabbar said. "Here was a guy who had more than just talent, but a guy who had a lot of drive to his game, a guy who had a lot of pride. He wasn't a total loser like so many of those guys that he hung around with, and you never thought he could turn out that way."

In 1969, the same year Jabbar was made a rookie millionaire by the Milwaukee Bucks, Manigault was arrested for possession of drugs and spent sixteen months of a five-year sentence at Green Haven Prison in Stormville, New York.

While still behind bars, Manigault's legend continued to grow. He was written about in *The City Game*, the classic book by Pete Axthelm about New York basketballers that caught the attention of Bill Daniels, owner of the Utah Stars of the American Basketball Association. Pete Vecsey, then writing for the *New York Daily News*, helped convince Daniels to give the Goat a shot at the big time.

When Manigault was released from prison in 1970 at the age of twenty-five, Daniels offered him a tryout. The Goat lasted midway through the preseason, and just before an eagerly anticipated exhibition game against Milwaukee and his boyhood chum Kareem, the Goat was cut.

"I drove Earl to the airport when he flew to Utah," said Willie Mangum, one of Manigault's former teammates at Benjamin Franklin. "But it was too late for him. His body had been through too much. He couldn't take the pace."

After spending his short time in Utah, Manigault shunned an offer to tour with the Harlem Globetrotters. "Nothing against the Globetrotters," he said. "But that just wasn't my style."

Manigault soon returned to Goat Park on 99th Street and Amsterdam Avenue to start up the Goat Tournament, created in Holcombe Rucker's memory with the goal of being as dedicated and committed to children as Rucker's. The Goat Tourney would fast become a prestigious summertime spectacular that over the years featured future NBA talents such as Reggie Carter, Bernard and Albert King, and Mario Ellie.

"I decided I wanted to give something back to the community because of all the respect and attention the people gave me over the years, even when I was suffering at my lowest point," Manigault said. "It was my way of saying thanks to all the people who stuck with me during my hard days—my drug days."

Despite his good intentions, the Goat's ugly drug habits resurfaced, and in 1977 he started messing with heroin again.

That summer, Manigault canceled the first day of the Goat Tournament, got in a car with friends, and headed for the Bronx.

"We had a plan to steal $6 million," said Manigault, who never revealed the details of that plan. "But we got busted. They figured I was the ringleader. I got two years."

After serving two years at the Bronx House of Detention and the state prison in Ossining, Manigault, who never married, took two of his sons—the youngest of his seven children—and moved to Charleston, far away from New York City and the temptation of drugs.

"I didn't want my sons to be greater junkies than I was," he says.

Manigault, however, would not last long in Charleston, as the guilt of abandoning his tournament and all the people who loved him in New York proved too much to ignore.

The Goat decided it was time to come home.

A Country Boy in the Big City

In the spring of 1968, a Greyhound bus came rumbling into the Port Authority terminal in New York City, carrying another young player with a world of potential. The busy terminal echoed with the sounds of squeaky hinges when the bus doors opened wide, letting out a six-foot-nine-inch twenty-year-old country bumpkin from Tryon, North Carolina, who knew as much about the big city as the big city knew about Harthorne Wingo. Almost nothing.

"Have you seen my aunt Martha?" Wingo asked one woman he had never seen before.

"The woman just kind of looked at me funny and shuffled off," Wingo said.

So he tried again.

"Have you seen my aunt Martha?" he asked an older gentleman he did not know.

"Who?" the older fella asked.

"Aunt Martha," said Wingo, a quizzical look painted on his face. "Do you know where she is?"

"Who the hell is Aunt Martha," the older man snapped, "and how the hell am I supposed to know where she is!"

His pockets empty and the brain beneath his straw hat filled with confusion, Wingo got scared, and then he got desperate. He began shouting in the busy terminal for someone, anyone, to help him.

"Please!" he barked. "Has anyone here seen my aunt Martha! Please . . ."

Having arrived from Smalltown, USA, where everyone knew everyone else, Wingo just figured everyone in Manhattan knew everyone else as well, including his aunt Martha.

"I had no idea how big New York was," Wingo told me years later. "When my aunt Martha finally arrived, and I told her what had happened, she just shook her head, looked up at me, and said, 'Young man, you got a lot of learning to do.' "

Having left behind a violent family that included his mother and fourteen brothers and sisters, Wingo was more than willing to learn anything in order to get a new life started. Having played just one year of junior college basketball at Friendship, a little-known institution of learning and hooping in South Carolina, playing roundball was hardly a career option.

In dire need of a paycheck, Wingo took a job wheeling around large racks of clothing in New York's garment center. In his spare time he played pickup basketball and, living in the Grand Concourse section of the Bronx, it wasn't long before he got wind of the action happening at nearby Rucker Park.

"When Wingy first walked into the park, everyone was like 'Who the hell is that?' " Joe Hammond said. "But he was a big body with some talent, and you could never have enough big bodies on your team."

Wingo joined Hammond's Milbank squad, and before long the two became close friends. Eventually, Hammond got Wingo a tryout with the Allentown Jets for which he played in the Eastern League, and word about the rail-thin, boney-kneed center's game began spreading up and down the East Coast.

By 1970, Wingo was one of Rucker Park's biggest stars. Dozens of professional scouts, cigarettes dangling from their mouths, stopwatches and notepads sitting on their laps, spread out in the stone bleachers to watch him play.

Late that summer, after being spotted at a pickup game in Greenwich Village, Wingo was offered a contract to tour locally with a show-team called the Harlem Wizards. Days after that contract expired, the phone rang in Wingo's tiny South Bronx apartment. It was Wingo's agent, telling him that the Knicks wanted his name on one of their contracts. Knicks scouts had watched him play at Rucker Park and at other playgrounds throughout the city, and liked what they saw.

"I jumped so high, I nearly hit my head on the ceiling," he said.

Wingo played for the Knicks from 1972 to 1976. Always the last man off of Red Holzman's bench, he would walk onto the Madison Square Garden floor long after games had been decided to chants of "Win-go, Win-go," the decibel levels at the Garden rising higher and higher, seemingly shaking the entire building on West 33rd Street.

Though he never received the playing time that more celebrated teammates like Walt Frazier, Earl Monroe, and Dave De-Busschere did, Wingo got an equal amount of champagne when the Knicks won the NBA championship following the 1972–73 season. "In those days," Frazier told me, "Wingy was on cloud nine with the rest of us."

Wingo enjoyed his best season in 1974–75, when he played in all eighty-two games for the Knicks, averaging 7.4 points per contest.

"I really felt I was coming into my own at that time," he said. "But then, just before the start of the next season, they went out and got Spencer Haywood from Seattle, which made me realize that I was pretty much through in New York."

After his career as a Knick ended, Wingo played in Italy for four seasons, Switzerland for one, and finished his career in Argentina, and then it all started to go wrong for New York City's favorite twelfth man.

Wingo encountered one misfortune after another. He separated from his wife and squandered all of his money on drugs, alcohol, fancy cars, and needy friends. Things got worse as Wingo developed arthritis in one of his hips. The day he hobbled into Harlem Hospital complaining of a bad hip, it was discovered that he had walking pneumonia.

I didn't know any of this. Few people did. Not until a frigid winter's day in 1991, when a drug dealer and numbers runner from my old Harlem neighborhood who knew me and knew I wrote for a number of local papers, took me to a run-down tenement brownstone on 130th Street and Madison Avenue, not far from Rucker Park, where the Wingo story first took flight.

"Wingo Har-thorne, he lives here," said Eddie, flopping Wingo's first and last names the way so many others who knew him had done during his heyday and do even still today. "You won't believe what happened to this guy."

I was between my first and second knock on the door when a man named Clemente King answered and told me that I was a few days behind Wingo's trail, that he had up and moved to a friend's house in Jersey City.

Clemente told me that Wingo, then forty-two, was trying to stay clear of his old haunts, his old friends, and his old habits, and that he had recently spent fifty-two days at the Institute of

Harthorne Wingo (*New York Times*)

Living, a private psychiatric hospital in Hartford, Connecticut, where he was treated for drug and alcohol abuse.

With a few helpful tips from Clemente, I was off to Jersey City the very next day, and found Wingo hiding out at the home of a friend who was in the sports memorabilia business. Wingo looked fairly well rested in a black nylon running suit and high-top sneakers, still fit enough to give Holzman and the Knick fans who loved him two more minutes of garbage time and another of those wide smiles during one of those "Win-go" curtain calls.

"I'm trying to put it all behind me," he said, choosing to look down and fiddle with some of the basketball cards that lay on the table in front of him instead of looking up at me while we spoke. "I'll admit, I still get high once in a while, and I still get tempted to go back to Harlem," he said. "But I'm going to stay here, far away from those people, and this time I'm going to clean up my act for good."

I asked Wingo why he had never sought the help of his old teammates, many of whom had moved on to more rewarding careers. I'll never forget how he closed his eyes tightly at that moment, the question piercing his heart.

"I was on the same team as those guys, but I was never, ever, in their league. They all had tremendous skills, a college education to fall back on, and a lot of contacts to help them out later in life. I didn't have all those things. They were big-time, and I was always just plain-old Wingy. I didn't want to dump my problems on any of them, it's kind of embarrassing. I just figured it's best to stay out of everyone else's way."

I told Wingo I had already called his old coach that morning, and that Red Holzman was stunned.

"I'm saddened to hear that he's in this situation," said Holzman, who died in 1998. "He was always a very conservative guy, the kind of guy you would never think could end up like this. But now it's time for him to come around and decide what he wants to do with his life."

And I had already called his teammates.

"I don't think he should stay away," Willis Reed said. "Hey, look, we've all made mistakes in our lives, but sometimes we have to swallow our pride and ask for a little help. If I'd never gotten any help, I know I wouldn't be where I am today."

As I relayed those sentiments to Wingo, large tears fell off his cheeks, splashing off the hardwood floor like thick raindrops. He got himself together and reached for a trading card with his picture on it.

He held the card up, pointed to his own picture, and said, "People used to ask this guy, 'If you're so good, then why are you sitting on the Knicks' bench?' But when I look back now, and I realize how many future Hall of Famers were on that team, well, hey, I'm just really proud of what that guy accomplished."

And then, finally, Harthorne Nathaniel Wingo looked up and asked me, "Do you think the guys in my old neighborhood, all those guys that watched me play up at the Rucker and at Madison Square Garden, do you think they still have this card?"

Wingo is back living in West Harlem. At the time of this writing, close friends said he was free of drugs and earning a living as a security guard at a downtown nightclub.

Chapter 4

DR. J. AND THE RUCKER
HEYDAY

J oe Hammond's star was soaring in the summers of 1971 and
1972, which marked the heydey of the Rucker Tournament,
a time when weekend crowds exceeded ten thousand, including a number of white faces in the large audiences who had
ventured into the deepest part of black Harlem to catch the
greatest basketball show on earth. "Virtually all of the spectators
were black," Dave Anderson, the Pulitzer Prize–winning columnist of the *New York Times* wrote of one Rucker crowd on August 12, 1972. "But there were a few white faces, scattered like
grains of salt in a pepper shaker."

At that time the tournament consisted of ten teams that
played a single, round-robin schedule of nine 40-minute games.
Though admission was free, pro players often made joint, out-
of-pocket donations to worthy causes in Harlem.

The best players during Rucker Park's glory years were all
New Yorkers. The best pros were Julius Erving, who grew up on
Long Island, and Nate Archibald, from the South Bronx.

"Playing in Rucker Park was an ego thing because there
were great players involved from both sides," Archibald said.
"In their hearts and souls the playground guys felt that they
didn't have the same opportunities as guys like myself and
Julius Erving did to get to the pros, and they thought they were

better than we were. So when I went out there, I had a lot to prove."

Erving grew up in the Roosevelt section of Long Island. So did Lee Jones, a longtime NBA referee who got his start officiating at Rucker games.

One day Earl Mosley, the junior varsity coach at Roosevelt High School, called Jones over to the gym to meet a young, energetic kid on his team who sported long arms and a tall afro hairstyle.

"You have to see this kid play," Mosley told Jones. "I think he's got some real potential."

Jones shook hands with fourteen-year-old Julius Erving, who was not yet being called the Doctor. (That nickname came shortly after, when Erving called a bright buddy at Roosevelt "Professor," and his buddy quickly responded: "And you are the Doctor.")

"He was a nice kid, not that tall yet," Jones said. "He was only about six two or six three at the time, and he was considered a very good player, not a great one—there's a difference. In fact, he did not even make the all–Long Island team as a high school senior."

Jones was there as a spectator for Erving's first-ever game at Rucker Park in the summer of 1969. "Julius had grown some six inches since high school," Jones said. "No one in the crowd, though, believed that kids from Long Island could really play basketball. Everyone always looked at it as strictly a city game.

"The first time Julius touched the ball, three defensive players converged on him," Jones recalled. "Suddenly, Julius just makes a sweeping move along the baseline, glides past all three of them, elevates, and, with his left hand, throws down a tremendous dunk.

Dr. J. dribbling up sideline at Rucker (*New York Times*)

"The crowd didn't even cheer because they were in complete shock," Jones said. "That was the first, and last, time they ever doubted that the kid from Long Island could play some ball."

That same summer, Willie Hall, who had been a star at Archbishop Molloy High School in Queens and later at nearby St. John's University, got his first glimpse of the nineteen-year-old kid from Long Island who was making a name for himself at the University of Massachusetts.

"This kid was tall and very lean with a gigantic afro, so big he looked like a lion on stilts when I first saw him walk into the park on 155th Street," said Hall, now sixty-four. "What me and everybody else in that park did not know was that this was one ferocious lion."

At the time, people were calling the young Julius Erving "The Claw" because of his huge hands and a long reach that enabled

Erving to dunk a basketball like no human being before him. "Erving's hands are so big," Pete Vecsey once wrote, "that he could palm Sunday."

Hall, whose pro career had ended after playing two seasons in Germany, was now teaming in the Rucker Pro division with Tom Hoover, himself winding down a five-year pro career in the NBA, two of them spent with his hometown New York Knicks.

Playing on a team called Sweet and Sour, which was named after a bar on 138th Street and Seventh Avenue, Hall and Hoover anxiously awaited the arrival of Erving, who was joining forces on a team called the Daily News All-Stars with Mike Riordan of the New York Knicks and soon-to-be pros Billy Paultz of St. John's and Ollie Taylor of Texas-Pan American.

"They were a great bunch of young players," Hall said. "They were in a lot better shape than we were, and they could run all day."

As the game began, Hoover tried to gain a psychological edge by taunting the younger player.

"But to his credit, Julius never said a word," Hall said. "Julius was like that up there. He was always the perfect gentleman."

With a capacity crowd cheering on the action, the six ten Hoover, who had not been guarding the six six Erving to that point, suddenly found himself smack in the middle of the lion's den after a switch, and now here he was, face to face with a young, hungry opponent eager to answer Hoover's taunts with the roar of his own mighty game.

Off the switch, Hoover, playing defense near his own basket, picked up Erving along the right baseline. Still yapping at Erving, Hoover had left a little bit of daylight between his body and the baseline, and Erving, smelling an opening to the tin, slipped past him, leaping high toward a netless rim. Hoover backpedaled furiously, his arms flailing desperately, but it was already too late—Julius was moving in for the kill.

As Erving glided toward the hoop, Hoover positioned himself directly beneath the basket, hoping to catch Erving on the descent. But this was a nonstop flight, and Erving was taking it across the other side of the rim.

"Remember that great reverse layup Doc pulled off against Magic Johnson and the Lakers in the NBA finals?" said Hall. "Well, this was the same type of reverse, except Doc finished it off with a powerful dunk."

But for Tom Hoover, the embarrassment did not end there. After Erving slammed the ball through the cylinder, it came crashing down on Hoover's head with such force, it dislodged the dentures in his mouth, and his full set of false teeth fell to the asphalt with a click-clacking sound that had the thousands in attendance, including players from both teams, howling in delight.

"You had to see those people going crazy that day. I mean they were really out to lunch after that," Hall said. "Shit, even Tom was cracking up after he picked up his teeth."

By playing against veterans like Hoover on the Rucker playground, Erving was shaping his game on every level. He was gaining the mental toughness he needed to help him survive at the next level. At the same time, he was able to use the tiny park as an experimental lab where he created the kinds of moves that would soon make him one of the world's most famous athletes.

"A lot of my dunks I learned at the Rucker," said Erving, who revolutionized the way the NBA game was played above the rim.

"At the Rucker, you had to come ready to do battle, to make your presence felt, to step up or get put down," he said. "You didn't have the luxury of playing an average game."

The Destroyer Runs Amok

By the time of Dr. J.'s spectacular dunk on Tom Hoover, Joe Hammond was all grown up, "an emancipated child" as Bob McCullough called him. At the age of nineteen back in 1969, The Destroyer had nary a minute of high school or college basketball under his elastic drawstrings, and yet he was already playing professionally with the Allentown Jets of the Eastern Basketball League. At Rucker Park he was indeed destroying the reputations of much older players and terrorizing players his own age, many of them college all-Americans who had come to the land of the Pied Piper to see what all the commotion was about.

"He was," said Julius Erving, "a very cagey player, very slick with the ball."

A mature coach lodged in a young man's body, Hammond could not be held down; no one defense had an answer for his high-rising, butterfly-release, and money-in-the-bank bank shot that Peter Vecsey called "maybe the greatest I've ever seen."

"He owned that backboard," Vecsey said of Hammond. "He could shoot from long range, take you off the dribble and dunk on you. These days if you're a guy like Del Curry or Glen Rice, you're a great shooter but you usually cannot take a man off the dribble, but Joe could do both. He loved to put on a show. Anything anybody could do on a basketball court, Joe could probably do it better, and I never saw a guy shoot more accurately outdoors, especially in the wind."

As Hammond's tricky ballhandling was turning hundreds of ankles on the asphalt and thousands of heads in the stone bleachers that overlook the tiny park, fewer and fewer people were calling him Dirty-Hand Joe. He was outgrowing that nickname and growing into another that fit his game like a glove: The Destroyer.

"The name fit, because this kid was simply destroying any and all competition," Howie Evans said. "He was so cool, like ice. His movements were so calculated, they were based on not what he could do but what players who were defending him couldn't do."

There were other facets of The Destroyer's game that simply fascinated Evans and anyone fortunate enough to have seen Hammond work his magic on the world's most magical basketball stage.

"He would never sweat," Evans said. "I don't care how hot it was. People used to think the guy was inhuman. Also, he was so totally relaxed on the court, like he was playing the game in his own living room.

"You could never get him distracted. You could throw him down to the ground and he would never say a word. And I can honestly say that in all the years I watched Joe play, I cannot remember him ever missing a free throw."

On the streets, Hammond was still making a fortune shooting craps, and now he found a way to invest his winnings.

"I started selling drugs when I was like nineteen or twenty," he said. "I took advantage of my popularity in that I knew everyone would want to buy off me, because everyone wanted to be around me. Before long I was making a small fortune."

Enough money at least to replace his duct-taped Pro Keds with dozens of pairs of spanking-new Converse sneakers. Any neighborhood kid whose sneakers were on life support got a brand-new pair or two from The Destroyer, "just as my own way of giving a little something back," he said.

On a rainy Saturday that summer, Joe Hammond laced up his Converses and headed for the Bronx. At Fordham University, The Destroyer would enjoy the most incredible, one-man basketball afternoon in the history of New York City.

As part of a unique doubleheader staged by Rucker officials, a game featuring a number of college all-Americans would be followed by a New York versus Philadelphia game that featured two rosters filled with only professional players.

In that first game, playing against the likes of Nate "Tiny" Archibald of Texas-El Paso and Dean "The Dream" Meminger of Rice High School and Marquette—both players were ticketed for the pros—The Destroyer took MVP honors with a spectacular 51-point performance. At one point in that contest, The Destroyer made six straight shots from what would now be considered three-point range. What made that string even more impressive was the fact that each of those baskets were banked in off the backboard, which was The Destroyer's signature shot.

Just about to head into a shower stall after that game, Hammond was approached by Teddy Jones, who coached the New York Pros.

Jones was well aware of established Liberty Bell talents like Earl Monroe and Archie Clark, and he was fearful of a new crop of talented young players sprouting up behind them in the Philly parks, dominant players and future pros of the 1970s like Joe "Jellybean" Bryant of La Salle (yes, his son is Kobe), Mike Sojourner of Utah, and Andre McCarter of UCLA.

Jones had begun to adopt a win-at-all-costs mentality, which is where The Destroyer came in.

"Hey Joe, do me a favor, man," Jones told Hammond. "Stick around for the next game. I think we could use an alternate guard."

Jones gave Hammond the only jersey he could find, a blue one, while all his other teammates wore red. Hammond joined a layup line that included Freddie Crawford of the New York Knicks, Connie Hawkins of the Phoenix Suns, and Pablo Robertson of the Harlem Globetrotters.

All the New York Pros began dunking during warmups, and Hammond began doing the same, except that The Destroyer had a little more flash to his flush than the big-leaguers, cradling the rock like a baby in his arms as he went airborne, then throwing it down with enough force to turn the heads of the players on Philly's layup line.

"I'll never forget this little white guy mopping the floor as we warmed up," Hammond said. "He knew I wasn't a regular on the pro team, but he said, 'You know what, kid, you're the best player in this whole damn gym. Go out there and show these old-timers what you're made of—give them a game they'll never forget.' "

Sitting at the end of the bench as the game began, Hammond watched as Philadelphia's Earl "The Pearl" Monroe and Archie Clark burned New York's backcourt.

"Monroe was just backing Pablo into the basket and scoring easily over him," Hammond said. "The next thing I know, Teddy is telling me to get in the game."

"Pick up Monroe," Jones told Hammond.

As the action continued, The Destroyer was pretty easy to locate. He was the only player on either team with a blue jersey, as New York wore red and Philadelphia white.

"On our first possession when I got into the game, I had the ball on the wing," Hammond recalled. "I threw it down low to Connie, who was not known for throwing the ball back outside once he got it deep in the paint. But Connie threw it right back at me and yelled, 'Young fella, do what you do best!' "

The Destroyer obliged the Hawk, head-faking Monroe and whipping past him and teammate Luke Jackson for what looked like a sure dunk. But The Destroyer, as always, was simply there to score and not to embarrass. Rising high, his elbow above the rim, Hammond just dropped the rock in the pond for an easy deuce.

"All of a sudden," Hammond said, "all of these great pros were suddenly looking to feed me the ball."

With Hammond leaping high over Philly defenders and burying his patented bank shot, New York began to take control on the scoreboard. Frustrated, Monroe and Clark began trying to trap The Destroyer in the backcourt. On one trap attempt late in the third quarter, as Monroe and Clark closed in on him from either side, Hammond spun as if he were heading out of bounds, spun back inbounds and whipped the ball around his back and through his legs in one fluid motion, splitting Monroe and Clark like bowling pins before dribbling out of traffic. By the time both defenders lunged for the ball, Hammond was past them, and Monroe and Clark bumped heads and fell to the hardwood, bringing the game to a halt for several embarrassing minutes.

When it was over, Hammond had 50 points and another trophy for his grandmother's museum. In one afternoon, in the space of three or four hours against the best basketball players on God's green earth, Joe "The Destroyer" Hammond had tallied 101 points.

And still, he wasn't even sweating.

Pee Wee in the Backcourt

The neighborhood team that Joe Hammond starred on was called Milbank, a community center and basketball power in West Harlem that featured some of the top players in the city. One of them was Richard "Pee Wee" Kirkland, an all-city point guard who attended Manhattan's Charles Evans Hughes High School in the late 1960s.

If Erving and Archibald were the two best pros competing at Rucker Park in the 1970s, then the two best playground stars were Hammond and Kirkland, the Walt Frazier and Earl Monroe of the playgrounds.

Kirkland enrolled at Kittrell Junior College in North Carolina, averaged 41 points, then went on to Norfolk State in Virginia. As a junior he teamed with Bob Dandridge, a future NBA

Pee Wee Kirkland dribbling on hardwood *(Pee Wee Kirkland)*

star, and was named to the Mideast Regional NCAA tournament team.

Kirkland was drafted by the Chicago Bulls in 1968 but never played in a game. A heated argument with the coach drove him back to the life he had known best—as a gangster on the streets of Harlem.

"The bitterness and pain comes not from what I didn't do," said Kirkland, "but how far I didn't go."

"I played on those Los Angeles Laker 'Showtime' teams in the 1980s with Magic Johnson, Kareem Abdul-Jabbar, and James Worthy," said Bob McAdoo, who played his college ball at North Carolina before he became a three-time NBA scoring champion in the 1970s. "But Pee Wee was orchestrating showtime at Norfolk State twenty years before that.

"Norfolk's philosophy was to push the ball up the floor and just fast-break everybody out of the gym," McAdoo said. "Pee Wee could fly. I'm telling you. He could dribble the ball baseline to baseline in about three seconds flat."

At the same time Kirkland was drafted by the Bulls, he was part of another team that made him a rich man—a band of jewel thieves, drug dealers, and money launderers. Despite a lucrative, flashy lifestyle, Kirkland decided to give the NBA a shot. It didn't last long. After a squabble over playing time with coach Dick Motta, and a failed opportunity with the San Diego Rockets of the ABA, Kirkland returned to his life of crime.

No matter how much money he was earning on the streets, Kirkland couldn't stay away from the game he loved. From 1968 to 1971, Kirkland, whose main professional rival was Tiny Archibald, teamed with Hammond and other Milbank stars like the "Elevator Man" Eric Cobb, and he of the enormous wingspan, Larry "Butterfly" Cheatham.

"For me, it was more than just a guy from the Boston Celtics playing against a guy from Milbank," Archibald said of his great rivalry with Kirkland. "It was Tiny Archibald, who grew up in the city, playing against Pee Wee Kirkland and Joe Hammond, who also grew up in the city. They brought their fans, and I brought mine. And I had to prove I was a formidable challenger to those guys.

"While I think Joe Hammond was maybe the best offensive player to ever come off the playgrounds," Archibald said, "I seriously believe that Pee Wee Kirkland was the best all-around player. I was fortunate to grow up in New York City because I got a chance to play against guys like Pee Wee and Joe. I had an NBA career, but I consider my experiences on the playground to be my summer professional career."

For three straight summers, Kirkland, playing in a league with some of the world's greatest professional players, was the scoring champion at Rucker Park.

"In those days, it was said that Pee Wee had a little satchel he'd bring to the park with him and slip under the bench before he stepped onto the court," said Pete Vecsey, a basketball columnist for the *New York Post* and television basketball analyst who coached in the park while covering the sport in those days for the *New York Daily News*. "People used to say Pee Wee had a gun in that satchel," Vecsey said. "So whenever he argued a call against my team. I'd always say, 'Yeah, you know, maybe you are right, Pee Wee, maybe you did get fouled on that play.' "

In 1971, word of Pee Wee's towering talents reached the ears of then–New York Knicks coach Red Holzman, who sent Kirkland a telegram inviting the playground phenom for a tryout with the Knicks.

But just days after Holzman's telegram arrived, Kirkland's

world began to go dark. He was arrested for conspiracy to sell narcotics and spent the next ten years in the Lewisburg Federal Penitentiary in Pennsylvania.

Yet even behind bars, the basketball legend of Pee Wee Kirkland continued to grow. There, Kirkland assembled one of the greatest basketball teams ever to play in the Anthracite Basketball League, a semipro circuit in central Pennsylvania that included prison teams. In one historic contest that made national headlines, Kirkland's team played against a team from Lithuania. Kirkland, an Al Capone with a crossover dribble, busted out, scoring 135 points in a 228–47 victory.

"IS KIRKLAND ANOTHER CHAMBERLAIN?" the *Philadelphia Inquirer* wondered. "LEWISBURG HAS A SHOOT-OUT," wrote the *Washington Post.*

But to the Lewisburg Hilltoppers, Kirkland's presence meant a lot more than simply scoring points and winning basketball games.

"The first thing prison does to a man is make him feel like a loser," Kirkland said. "I took thirteen guys who had no confidence in themselves, no hope for their futures, and I gave them something to strive for, something to be proud of."

Kirkland, who is also believed to be the first player in New York City to perform a 360-degree turn on a move to the basket, has now done a 180 in life. Now fifty-seven, Kirkland has for the past nine years run the School of Skillz at the Central Baptist Church on 92nd Street and Amsterdam Avenue, where more than two hundred youngsters each weekend learn the basics of the game "from the neck up," Kirkland says, "the way it's supposed to be played."

Kirkland's schoolyard reputation brought other opportunities, and his leadership skills and charisma helped him take advantage of them. Professor Kirkland has taught two classes at Long Island University on the philosophy of basketball coaching, and he still gives motivational speeches at schools around the country. He has appeared in numerous radio and television commercials for Nike, and along the way coached the prestigious Dwight School in Manhattan to an Independent Schools state championship. Pee Wee even had a small part in the big-screen movie *Above the Rim*, in which he played a basketball scout. The movie, directed by Jeff Pollack, starred the late Tupac Shakur, Duane Martin, and the actor known as Leon.

"Everything is timing," said Kirkland, who was also known as the "Stick Man," a nickname that described his long, thin body. "Thirty years ago I was part of the problem. Thirty years later, I'm a part of the solution.

"All those years in prison, I thought about all the people who had lived their dreams through my life, the people who wanted to see me go into the NBA," he said. "I knew that the only way to repay those people was to one day work with kids, because somewhere out there, there's another Pee Wee Kirkland, and until that kid turns his life around, I will always feel his pain."

Clash of the Titans

Cal Ramsey is certain as to who the best of the very best players were in the long history of Rucker Park.

"The two greatest Rucker players of all time were Julius Erving and Joe Hammond," Ramsey said. "I think Joe was that good. He was the one playground player who always stuck out in my mind. You hear a lot of talk throughout the years about 'this guy was that' and 'this guy was this,' but I watched a lot of those other playground guys play, and there was an awful lot of exaggeration attached to their games.

"Joe, he could flat out play," Ramsey said. "He was a six four two-guard who could shoot and slash, a combination of Allan Houston and Latrell Sprewell. He was a bona fide player who could have been an NBA All-Star, and there's no doubt in my mind about that."

And there's no doubt in the minds of those in the standing-room-only crowds, many bunched atop fences and roofs like pigeons, many others watching from high up on the viaduct leading to the 155th Street Bridge for a birds-eye view of the rivalry between Hammond and Erving that came to a head on a summer's day in 1971.

"We want Joe!" the crowd chanted on that historic day. "We want Joe!"

They stomped their feet as they chanted, but their local hero was nowhere to be found. The chanting continued to fill the Harlem air as players from both teams readied themselves for what everyone expected to be the most storied playground matchup ever: a once-in-a-lifetime duel between Julius Erving, the great Dr. J., and his playground nemesis, Joe "The Destroyer" Hammond.

On a steamy afternoon that fathers still tell their sons about, Erving, the Michael Jordan of the bell-bottom generation, led a team of professional players called the Westsiders into the park to square off against Hammond's Milbank squad, which included his dynamic backcourt partner, Pee Wee Kirkland.

The six six Dr J. was about to burst onto the pro scene with the Virginia Squires of the ABA. He was teamed that day with fellow pros Charlie Scott, Billy Paultz, Mike Riordan, and Brian Taylor, all hungry to win the ultimate playground prize: a Rucker championship and the lifetime of basketball bragging rights that go with it.

"The operating table is ready," the league's courtside announcer, Plucky Morris, blared over the public address system as thousands of fans filled the park, many perching themselves on tree limbs and rooftops for a better look at the action, "and the Doctor has his scalpel out."

The crowd gave Harlem's version of a Roman Colosseum roar. A handful of the Harlem faithful had bright orange bracelets wrapped around their wrists. These were patients at nearby Harlem Hospital who had rushed to the park to catch the action.

On the other layup line was Milbank, a neighborhood team composed mainly of playground phenoms with colorful nicknames straight out of the World Wrestling Federation. The Milbank players looked over their shoulders for Hammond, but their six three shooting god was AWOL. The Milbank players stalled as long as possible, but the referees insisted the game go on as scheduled. Just minutes into the contest, Erving and company delighted the Rucker faithful with a lightning-quick transition game, finishing fast breaks with jaw-dropping swoops to the hoop and thundering dunks. "The Doctor is operating," Plucky Morris said as Erving head-faked Milbank's Elevator Man, Eric Cobb, whipping past him and embarrassing him with a two-handed flush that nearly shook some fans out of the trees. "The operation was a success," said Morris, "the patient died."

By halftime, the Westsiders had built a comfortable, double-digit lead.

Just before the start of the second half, as players again warmed up on their respective layup lines, a park mascot known only as "Happy" scooted around the blacktop with a large squeeze-bottle filled with wine, and poured the sweet red stuff into the open mouths of any player or fan who waved him over. As Happy was making his rounds, a savage roar ripped through the crowd, and fans in attendance began clapping their hands, stomping their feet, and craning their necks.

Across Eighth Avenue, Hammond, who said he missed the first half because he was shooting craps in a nearby social club, was getting out of a limousine. Swarmed by hundreds of autograph seekers and well-wishers, The Destroyer made a move for the court, and then, suddenly, Hammond said later, "the crowd parted for me the way the Red Sea parted for Moses." Hammond rushed onto the court, slipped off his dress clothes to reveal a tank top and shorts, and shouted to no one in particular, "I'm here, coach, I'm here!"

With the crowd drifting into the outer limits of hysteria, the second half began with Scott guarding Hammond. Soon after, Erving was ordered to lock down Hammond, and offensive fireworks filled the day.

"Everything we gave them, they gave it right back," said Pete Vecsey, then the Westsiders' coach. "All of us watched that day as Hammond, a kid who had surfaced from the cracks of Harlem, became a superstar."

On Milbank's first offensive possession after The Doctor locked horns with The Destroyer, Hammond called for a clearout, meaning he wanted his teammates to scatter so he could take The Doctor mano-a-mano. "Once the crowd heard me call for a clearout," Hammond said, "the place went hysterical."

A strong leaper who rarely dunked during his playing days, Hammond faked a move to his left from the foul line and went right with The Doctor in hot pursuit. Deep down the lane, both players elevated, and Hammond, with Erving literally stuffed in his jersey, took The Doctor for a little ride up north, windmilling a jam over The Doc's tall afro and down through the basket.

"The crowd went off the hook, and Doc was screaming to the ref, saying I pushed off on him," said Hammond. "But the ref said, 'No way, Julius, if anything, the foul was on you.'"

When the smoke cleared, Hammond said he had 50 points, earning most valuable player honors, and The Doctor 39, as the Westsiders pulled out the victory in triple overtime.

But there are several conflicting versions of the confrontation between Hammond and Dr. J.

Erving also agrees that the Westsiders won the contest, but remembers Hammond playing the entire game, not guarding him one-on-one the whole time, and not scoring as many as 50 points.

The Westsiders coach, Pete Vecsey, also dismisses Hammond's 50-point total, saying he remembers both players scoring roughly 40 points apiece.

Ernie Morris, the Rucker historian who was in the park that day, relayed what he had seen: "Both players were great, and Joe did have a great game, and he did come late, but saying that he scored fifty points against Dr. J. is a complete fabrication."

"You must remember," said Morris, "that Dr. J. was at the height of his run at that time. He was killing everybody back in the day. Now Joe held his own against Doc, but fifty in a half against the best player in the world? Get the hell out of here!"

Based on numerous interviews I've done throughout the years regarding the game, I've concluded that the facts surrounding the mythical battle have indeed been somewhat distorted in Hammond's favor.

While a great many people in Hammond's corner swear The Destroyer piled up 50 on Dr. J., the people who were a part of the action that day, including Hammond's backcourt partner Pee Wee Kirkland put his scoring total in the low 40s. And while it is pure fact that Hammond had more 50- and 60-point games in Rucker Park than any other player, it is difficult to imagine that he could pile up those numbers not only against a player of Erving's caliber, but against the caliber of collective talent on the Westsiders. And even if the defense was Swiss cheese that day, a 50-point total from Hammond in less than a full game would have meant that Kirkland and company, gunslingers themselves, would have hardly touched the ball—and Kirkland says he finished with 38 points in that historic showdown.

But more important than Hammond's final point total is the reputation of the man he allegedly destroyed that day. Yes, during the course of that battle, Hammond and Dr. J. did meet on an occasional switch. But for the most part, scores of honest eyewitnesses remember Hammond being guarded mostly by the Westsiders' Charlie Scott and several other players, while Milbank's Vincent White was given the dubious task of guarding the good Doctor. Considering the fact that Hammond played mostly shooting guard and Erving played mostly small forward, that scenario has always made more sense to me.

Kirkland himself, the man feeding Hammond the ball that day, insists that Hammond's big day did not come at Erving's expense. "Joe needs to stop talking this bullshit," Kirkland said flatly. "Joe was a great player, and scoring fifty or sixty points was not unlikely for a guy with his talent, he proved that time after time, but he didn't do it that day, and certainly not against Julius."

"I remember that game like it was yesterday," said Kirkland. "Joe had forty-three points that day, and I remember him scoring a basket or two when Julius was guarding him, but the rest of those points came against other people. In the end, I think a story like this hurts Joe more than it helps him because people come away with the impression that he had to make up a story to be a great player. But Joe never needed that kind of hype because he was one of the all-time greats out there."

And yet, Hammond's feathers still get a bit ruffled when anyone disputes what he still insists was a 50-point masterpiece.

"Whether Doc or anyone else remembers or not, I still won the MVP in that game," Hammond said. "Don't nobody doubt that. They gave me the MVP over all of those pro players because I deserved it. I scored more, I did more, and I excelled more than they did in that game."

The Sitdown

I had been trying to arrange a little one-on-one with the great Dr. J. for the better part of a decade, trying to set the record straight, once and for all, about his legendary showdown with Joe Hammond.

Now here we were face-to-face, in an Orlando, Florida, hotel room in 1999, almost thirty years after the big game. Despite the flecks of gray dancing in his hair, The Doctor still looked fit enough to get out on a fast break and assault a rim. Appearing to have the body fat of lettuce, his biceps bulging through a white business shirt, the forty-eight-year-old Erving had defied Father Time the way he once defied gravity.

"Just in case you're wondering," he assured me, "I can still dunk it."

Before long, we got to talking about his days at Rucker Park, about "some of the things I haven't talked about in years," as Erving put it.

For the first five years of his professional career, during which he played with the Virginia Squires and New York Nets of the ABA, The Doctor was the brightest star in Holcombe Rucker's constellation.

"It's a time in my life that is near and dear to me," he said. "It was a great journey for me of discovery, of learning more than I had previously known about the game. I didn't know how long I was going to play or how good I was going to be. I didn't know a lot of things, but being able to play in the summers up there was a great journey of confidence-building and understanding more than I had known in the previous twenty-one years."

Erving, who left the University of Massachusetts as a sopho- more in 1971, was an acrobatic, professional scorer from 1971 to 1987. His graceful strides, arsenal of innovative moves to the hoop, and thundering dunks did a lot more than just wow ca- pacity crowds. The Doctor's smooth operating style helped en- hance the image of his sport, allowing it to soar to immeasurable artistic heights during his professional heyday, ultimately push- ing professional basketball to a level of popularity it had not pre- viously known.

"Most star players in high school are thirty-point scorers, in college they become twenty-point scorers, and in the pros, they get ten points a game," Erving said. "I was the opposite, the ex- ception. I was actually a better pro than amateur. I was among the top one hundred players in high school, but I wasn't the best. I was among the top forty players in college, but I wasn't the best. But in the pros, I was able to reach the pinnacle of suc- cess and become the best player in the game."

An All-Star selection in each of his sixteen pro seasons, Erving credits those valuable minutes he played at the Rucker for much of his success at the big-league level.

"The league and the tournament and the challenges there had a lot to do with it, it let me have the freedom," said Erving, his eyes opening wide. "For me, it was an empowering experience. I loved coming back to the park summer after summer.

"In high school or college, I never went out and scored forty, fifty, or sixty points," he said, "but in the parks, you start rockin' and rollin' during a forty-eight-minute game and the next thing you know, when the smoke clears, somebody is bringing out the stat sheets and saying, 'Oh man, you got sixty today!'

"Sixty? I never got sixty before," Erving said. "But a lot of it had to do with the environment and the freedom and the fact that it was showtime and the shackles were being taken off. You're letting it all hang out, and you're playing the game at another level, and the guys you're playing against are bringing stuff out of you that maybe guys you played with before, in the organized set, didn't bring out of you.

"I probably could have scored sixty in college," said Doc, "but nobody brought it out of me."

The good Doctor recalled one particular game at UMass when he was feeling the freedom.

"I had thirty-nine in college once, and the coach pulled me out and said, 'I want you to break the school record when you're a senior,'" Doc jokingly recalled. "But I never had a senior year. He was playing God. But it wasn't like that in the parks. If you had sixty, people were yelling, 'Get seventy! Get eighty!'"

Erving, who retired with Philadelphia after the 1986–87 season, winning a pair of ABA championships with the New York Nets and an NBA title with the 76ers along the way, recalled his first days of training camp with the Virginia Squires. He was just a rookie, but the battle scars he earned at Rucker Park helped him stand head and shoulders above everyone else in Squires' camp in Petersburg, Virginia.

"I actually played in the Rucker the summer before I played for the Squires," he said. "I remember the second day of scrimmaging at training camp. It was like an open tryout with about thirty-five guys in the gym. They had set up different ten-man teams to scrimmage. I was running hard, real hard, and dunking on guys. These guys were getting mad, so the trainer went over to the coach and told him to sit me down. He told the coach, 'Take him out because one of these guys is going to hurt him.'

"I was running hard because that was a carryover from my Rucker days," Erving explained. "Having played in the Rucker, I only knew one way to play as a young pro, and that was hard. It was a confidence gained in believing you could do it. I'd already played against [almost] seven-footers like Connie Hawkins, Tom Hoover, and Harthorne Wingo in the same place where Wilt had played, and I thought then, 'If I come down the lane and go up and then they jump to block it, and if I can still hang there for a while and they hit me on the elbow while I'm throwing it down, well, I can do that on the other guys, too, because these guys are already pros.'

"So my confidence was sky-high," Erving said. "I felt invincible."

Erving, now the executive vice president of the Orlando Magic, also sits on the board of directors of four public companies. Basketball gave Dr. J. the wings to soar to those places, and playing at Rucker Park, he said, created a lot of wind beneath those wings.

"All that competition, all that love those people gave us, it was a good, growing experience for a boy from the suburbs," he said. "Each summer, playing in the park was my urban experience, and culturally, I still feel very connected to that."

We finally got around to Joe Hammond, and the disputed 50 points.

"Not true," said The Doctor.

"Not true?" I shot back.

"Absolutely no truth to it," Doc snapped.

The Doctor told me that he remembered playing against Hammond, but that there was no dramatic halftime entrance by The Destroyer, that Harlem's shooting god did not score 50 points, and that the two players did not guard each other for the entire game.

"Let me start by saying that Charlie Scott showed me the ropes up at Rucker," Erving said. "We were like Batman and Robin, and since it was his team, I was Robin. So any matchup we had was always Charlie versus Joe, Charlie versus Pee Wee, or Charlie versus whoever. But because I became the more significant pro athlete, suddenly the stories get turned around like it was me versus somebody, when that really wasn't the case.

"In all of the six years I played at Rucker, I saw Joe once," Erving said, "and he and Charlie had a little thing. When I first heard the story, I was trying to recall that game. I was thinking, 'Did that really happen?' "

He smiled a smile that filled the room: "I called Peter Vecsey, and I asked him, 'Did that guy get fifty on me, or was that on Charlie?' "

(Vecsey said he is not surprised by Doc's defensive stance: "I think that with the stuff being written about Joe, that he could get forty on Julius, that people are putting Joe in the same breath," Vecsey said. "Julius was voted one of the fifty greatest NBA players. His legend is solid. It's real.

"But," Vecsey added, "this was the summertime, and the fact of the matter is that Joe could get forty on him. Julius was never known to play great defense. But he doesn't like it when you say that Michael Jordan is better, so don't tell him that Joe Hammond is better—you have to understand where he's coming from.")

There was, Erving said, one truth to the Westsiders' storied matchup with Milbank.

"We beat them," he said. "I don't know exactly what Joe's stats were, I just know we took care of business, that was the main thing. We put on a show, and they put on a show. In fact, they were the masters of putting on a show."

The Doctor did admit, however, that Hammond was a pretty good operator himself back in Harlem's hallowed days.

"I thought he was pretty good," Erving said. "He was slick with the ball, had a good shot, and was very cagey. He was the best player on that team, I'll concede that. He was a true play-ground legend. Thirty-nine in the parks? That's not such a big night, but fifty in a half?

"Look," Erving said, "I'm sensitive to the fact that Joe and some other playground legends might need something like that, and if it's a little bit at my expense, so what? I can roll with it. But if I get an audience, I need to say what really happened, I need to tell the true story."

The Doctor explained to me that in the winter of 1990, when he read my account in the *New York Times* about his legendary battle with The Destroyer, he was careful not to react too harshly.

"I didn't go out of my way to seek an audience," he said, "be-cause sometimes, when you're trying to tell the true story versus something that's put out there, it sounds a little like sour grapes, and all you do is give the story more life."

Erving added that no matter how history writes about his meeting with The Destroyer or any other spine-tingling tale told before or after, it can never fully describe what playing on Holcombe Rucker's stage meant to a man who would become the greatest basketball attraction in the world. He only hopes he was able to give as much as he got.

"I felt as though I was taking a lot in terms of the competition and all the confidence that was being built, but I was giving as well," he said. "I was a professional player. I didn't get paid for being there, so the exchange really had to be sweat equity, strain and exhibition of talent in exchange for feeding off of what I was receiving.

"I don't know whether I gave more or took more," Doc concluded, "but I felt as though it became a good deal."

Erving said it was unfortunate that Rucker's grand stage was not hosting as many classic clashes between pros and their playground counterparts as it did in the days when the top of his afro seemed to reach the Harlem sky.

"In my day, Rucker Park was seen by guys coming up as a platform to prove themselves," he said. "With a lot of that gone, maybe you've lessened the possibility of legends being created— even if those legends are based on fact or fiction."

The one thing that no one can dispute, however, is the fact that the Erving-Hammond matchup, that once-in-a-lifetime collision between the very best of hardwood and blacktop in the summer of 1971, officially put the Rucker Tournament on the basketball map, giving it a name almost as big as The Doctor's signature afro hairstyle.

"For the pros to be there during that window of time in the

138

ASPHALT GODS

summer was probably the thing that let it gain some national and international recognition," said Erving, recalling the early 1970s, when he shined brightest in a galaxy of NBA stars who lit up the tiny park.

"But for the community, the park has always been a fixture," he added. "The characters who were a part of creating the whole experience shouldn't be belittled by just the fact that pros visited there. It was much more than that."

Always blessed with great court vision, Dr. J. could see that the biggest name on the biggest of basketball afternoons was not on the blacktop or in the stands. Holcombe Rucker, in fact, had already been dead for eight years, but his legacy was still growing, his influence still changing the face of basketball, New York City, and a large slice of American culture.

The Mountain Comes to Mohammed

In much the same, speedy way that word of a young, quick-drawing gunslinger from the Wild West would travel through cowboy country, The Destroyer's reputation spread from coast to coast following his legendary shootout with Dr. J. and company in the Rucker Final of 1971.

That same year, the Los Angeles Lakers of Wilt Chamberlain, Jerry West, and Elgin Baylor were so intrigued with the possibility of adding Joe Hammond to their roster, the team brought the mountain to Mohammed. The Lakers, who were in New York to play the Knicks, held a special tryout for the six-foot-three-and-a-half-inch playground legend.

"He was as well known as guys from the Knicks were at that time," said Lou Carnesecca, then piloting the New York Nets of the ABA. "People talked about him like he was a god.

"How great was he?" Carnesecca asked out loud. "It would take pages to fill. It's difficult to imagine if you've never seen him play, but at a young age, he already had the experience and the

Joe Hammond, ripping down a rebound in Milbank T-shirt
(Joe Hammond)

technique that make players great. He had no fear. He'd play anyone, anywhere, anytime."

Though Hammond had not played high school or college basketball, reams and reams of copy had been written about him in those Pennsylvania towns where people saw Hammond and the Allentown Jets play basketball.

"The 6-4, 180-pounder is one of the most exciting players in the game," reads the last sentence of Hammond's biography in the Jets' 1971 media guide.

The Lakers arranged the tryout through Howie Evans, who was the closest thing Hammond had to an agent. Evans took The Destroyer down to Pace University.

"To the best of my knowledge, that has never happened before," Vecsey said. "That's how talented a player Joe was. The Lakers actually came to him."

At the gym, Evans introduced Hammond to then-Lakers coach Bill Sharman and general manager Fred Schaus. Sharman quickly inserted Hammond into the middle of a shooting drill that included Chamberlain, West, Baylor, Gail Goodrich, and Leroy Ellis.

As was one of his routines in practice, Sharman then split his players up on each side of the court. Big men on one side, little men on the other. The goal of each group was to win the drill by making as many consecutive shots as possible. As expected, the little guys always defeated their taller teammates in this one particular exercise.

This time, however, Sharman added a little wrinkle to the drill, placing Hammond in with Chamberlain, Ellis, and the rest of the big boys.

"Joe made eighteen shots in a row," Evans said. "Wilt started going crazy. He started yelling, 'Shoot, young boy, keep shooting!'

"Sharman was trying to play it cool," Evans said. "He was walking around, trying not to look so much in Joe's direction."

Eventually, Sharman had the players switch sides, and Hammond rattled off another fourteen baskets in a row.

"When Coach Sharman ended his practice, he asked me if Joe could stick around a bit," Evans said. "He told everyone else to get dressed, and kept Joe and one other guy out there to play a one-on-one.

"Well, Joe starts killing this guy, I mean humiliating him," Evans said. "This guy finally gets so mad, so desperate, he throws Joe down to the ground. Finally, Sharman walks up to his guy and says to him, 'Forget it, you can't beat this kid.' "

Evans remembers the faces of Chamberlain and several other Lakers all staring at the action through a small window that looked into the gym. Some of them had grins on their faces; others wore expressions of total shock.

And Evans remembers the expression on the face of the player Hammond had just taken on a tour of Harlem.

"Pat Riley," said Evans, "he was pretty mad that day. I'll never forget it."

Shortly thereafter, the Lakers contacted Evans and told him they would be selecting Hammond in the NBA's hardship draft, and asked Evans if he could send the appropriate paperwork to the team's office in Los Angeles.

"But Joe had never been to school or work, so he really had no records anywhere," Evans said. "In my office I had a huge box filled with hundreds of college recruitment letters that were never opened, and a number of unsigned contracts sent to me from semipro and professional teams, all of whom were hoping I'd talk Joe into playing for them. But the only people who ever saw Joe play were the people who came to the parks, so as far as the NBA was concerned, and most everyone else who had never seen him play, Joe Hammond never really existed."

Evans gathered what records he could and forwarded them out west, and then history was made. The Destroyer was selected along with Nate Williams of Utah State (selected by the Cincinnati Royals), Tom Payne of Kentucky (Atlanta), Cyril Baptiste of Creighton (San Francisco), and Phil Chenier of California (Baltimore).

The Destroyer was offered a fifty-thousand-dollar, one-year contract by the Lakers, but "Joe didn't care about basketball or the Lakers or anything else," said Pete Vecsey, "because he was too busy making money on the streets."

"They thought they were offering the world to this poor kid from the ghetto, but I didn't need the money," Hammond said. "I was dealing drugs and shooting dice on the street for so long, I had over two hundred thousand dollars stashed in my apartment by the time the Lakers made their offer. I was making thousands of dollars a year selling marijuana and heroin. What was I going to do with fifty thousand?

"I was making guys like Dr. J. look silly," Hammond added. "And some of those guys were making big money, $200,000 or $250,000 a year. I told the Lakers that I deserved what those guys were making because I was better than most of them, but they refused to pay me. Then I asked them for a no-cut, guaranteed contract, and they refused me again. They couldn't understand how this poor boy from the slums could be playing hardball with them. And of course, I couldn't tell them why."

Although contract negotiations were going nowhere, the Lakers still invited Hammond to play in their Los Angeles summer league. According to Evans, they offered Hammond three hundred dollars per game, a house to live in while he was there, and a chauffeur-driven car, since Hammond did not drive.

"Then Joe asked if he could bring all of his friends from the neighborhood, and the Lakers said no," Evans said. "Joe wanted to show his buddies a good time, especially the ones who'd stuck by him when he had nothing, so when the Lakers said no, Joe just said 'Forget it.'"

At the time, Evans himself owned an Eastern League franchise called the Garden State Colonials. The best player on the Colonials roster was Elnardo Webster, the former St. Peter's star who spent parts of the 1971–72 season with New York and Memphis of the ABA.

Evans reached out to The Destroyer.

"Joe became our highest-paid player," said Evans, "but the only time he ever showed up was to play Allentown, because they had so many good players. He never showed up for any of the other games."

The Destroyer drifted back to the comforts and celebrity of his own neighborhood, refusing to listen to those who told him he had made a huge mistake in turning down the Lakers.

"People would ask me how I could refuse to get down with star players like Wilt and Jerry West," Hammond said. "But I owned a piece of a nightclub, two apartments, and a house. You want to know how rich I was? I owned two fancy cars—and I couldn't even drive."

After Hammond spurned the Lakers, Carnesecca and the Nets came calling. The coach arranged a special meeting with

Hammond at his favorite Italian restaurant, Dante's, which is walking distance from the St. John's campus.

"He was slender, but he had the body of a player. You could see the athleticism was there," Carnesecca said. "Joe had tremendous skills, all of which he learned on the streets, and a great, great future. He was a precursor to Magic Johnson and guys like that.

"From a physical standpoint," said Carnesecca, "Joe had all the skills. He also had the ability to make his teammates look better out on the court. He was a typical New Yorker. He could drive and split through three players, and when another defender came over to block his shot, he'd just dish it off. He could handle the ball, and he could always see the next play unfolding on the court. You can't teach that, it's a gift."

The Nets roster was also filled with some of the world's most talented players, including a young Rick Barry, Billy Melchionni, and Ollie Taylor. "Ollie, he would jump so high, he wouldn't come down for a week," Carnesecca said.

The coach offered Hammond a three-year, no-cut contract, $30,000 the first year, $35,000 in the second year, and $40,000 in the final year. And yet, before the penne got cold, The Destroyer said softly, "I really appreciate your kind offer, coach, but I'm not interested in signing."

"That was a lot of money in those days," Carnesecca said. "But the ABA was a vagabond league at the time, so I guess he felt he could do better, and that maybe the situation wasn't right for him."

To an extent, Carnesecca understood how Hammond could not escape the orbit of his own basketball world.

"The guy was from the streets," Carnesecca said. "He was

their guy, their local hero who never left them. He could still run for mayor up there and win. And believe me, there was a lot of pressure on guys like Joe playing up at the Rucker in those days, because a lot of those games, well, let's just say they were considered the big money games."

Dean Meminger, the former Knick who grew up in New York and competed against Hammond in the Rucker League, echoed Carnesecca's praise for Hammond. "Joe was as talented a player at the ages of eighteen, nineteen, and twenty as anybody in the city, or in the country, at that time," Meminger said. "But Joe didn't go through the system, and that hurt his marketability. It's often very difficult to gauge how good someone is based on their performance in the playgrounds."

But based on those playground performances, some pros knew exactly how good The Destroyer really was.

Said Evans: "It got to the point, I swear, where some professional players would drive up to the gyms where the big games were being played and ask people hanging out in the hallways, 'Is Joe in there?' If the answer was yes, they'd turn around, jump back in their cars, and go home."

The Lakers and Carnesecca's Nets had a pretty good idea of just how phenomenal Hammond would be on the college and professional levels had he allowed himself to be coached.

"Just think if Joe had been able to have all those skills refined," Carnesecca said, "if some coach gave him a little touch here and a little touch there. It's like a person with a great voice. You can have a great voice, but you still need a maestro to refine that voice, to give it a pitch and a tone. He would have been a great college player, an all-American, and an outstanding ten- to fifteen-year pro."

Carnesecca, whose Nets made it to the 1972 ABA finals but never won a red, white, and blue title, was asked if that piece of history might have been written differently had The Destroyer joined forces with him that day at Dante's.

"If Joe walked into my office right now, at this very moment," said Carnesecca, pounding his desk for emphasis, "I'd just look at him and say, 'Joe, you could have made me a contender.'"

Chapter 5

UNDER THE LIGHTS

I n the summer of 1972 the Harlem Professional Basketball League added a glitzy twist to its weekend competitions in an effort to accommodate droves of arriving players and overflow crowds. In addition to Saturday and Sunday afternoon games, Friday night games under lights were added. The festive flavor was enhanced by soul music that filled the park, another Rucker tradition carried on by deejays, fans, and players who currently prefer hip-hop, rap, and a dash of classic disco music with their local hoop theater. While the weekend extravaganzas were a blast, the crowded conditions often worried police and Parks Department officials. In June of that year, fans desperate for a view of the games broke into a nearby school and walked to the roof of the building to watch. Police from the 32nd Precinct were called in to remove the spectators.

The show, of course, went on, and the ever-increasing level of competition had hoop fans everywhere buzzing. Certainly the pros were impressed.

"There's really good, consistent competition up here," Riordan, the former Knick, said in a *New York Times* interview in the summer of '71. "They really know their basketball too, and if you come up here out of shape, you'll find out about it—some of the guys you never heard of give you the most trouble."

That same summer of 1972, with Rucker action literally bursting at the seams and thriving on its enormous popularity, something began to go painfully wrong in Harlem's version of hoop heaven. Walt Robertson of the Harlem Globetrotters, Pablo's brother, injured his knee playing on the asphalt surface and had to have an operation. The league, which did not charge admission but did have insurance, had to pay three thousand dollars for Robertson's operation. Then a player named Charlie Vasz broke his ankle playing and Elnardo Webster broke a toe. Then Vaughn Harper, who would later become one of New York's better-known deejays, broke a leg in two places. Austin Carr, a great player from Notre Dame, hurt his knee at the park, and though he went on to have a decent career with the Cleveland Cavaliers, he was never really the same player he was in college. With each injury, the league's insurance policy grew more expensive. Finally the league could no longer afford to pay for adequate coverage.

"We had to move the tournament indoors," Bob McCullough recalls.

The next two years, the Rucker Tournament was moved to City College on 138th Street and Convent Avenue, but the hardwood floors and fluorescent lights that subbed for the asphalt surface and overhead streetlamps stripped the showcase of its true identity.

"It just wasn't the same," said Lee Jones, the longtime NBA referee who worked some of those games. "The crowds were just not the same indoors, and the tournament was missing that certain kind of street kid, that Joe Hammond or Pee Wee Kirkland, who hung around the parks, waiting around for his fifteen minutes of fame."

By this time, copycat leagues complete with visiting pros had sprouted up in major cities all over America, as summer tourneys were held in places like Philadelphia and Washington (both of which sent all-stars to play the Harlem Professionals), Detroit, Chicago, Newark, Louisville, and Buffalo. And much of the same was happening at the high school and collegiate levels, as the Holcombe Rucker Community League became the blueprint for basketball youth leagues throughout the nation.

A Training Ground for Refs

With Rucker action having moved indoors temporarily, the focus shifted to the hardwood, where one of Joe Hammond's Allentown teammates, a Brooklyn kid named Ronnie Nunn, was fast making a name for himself.

An all-city player at Brooklyn Tech who went on to star at George Washington with Walt Szczerbiak, Nunn excelled for two basketball seasons from 1972 to 1974 in the old Eastern League, and was also a star player in Mexico, averaging 21 points per game for León, a professional team playing in the state of Guanajuato.

After the six three, smooth-shooting point guard led León to a championship over San Luis Potosí in 1973, the overseas operator patched through a call from the Denver Nuggets, who were interested in having Nunn try out for their ballclub.

Nunn became the last cut of the Nuggets that preseason and went back to play in Mexico, waiting for yet another long-distance call. While he waited, Nunn contracted hepatitis—"I think I ate a bad hot dog," he said—and was still in recovery mode when New York Knicks coach Red Holzman dialed him up the following season.

"I understand you were supposed to be a player for Denver last year," Holzman told Nunn. "I'd like you to come to New York and try out with the Knicks."

Nunn, still sick, flew north anyway.

"But I couldn't pass the physical," he said. "I guess it just wasn't in the cards for me."

When each of his two seasons ended in Mexico, Nunn came home to play in the Rucker Tournament. He had watched spectacular games there while playing at Brooklyn Tech in the mid-1960s—"I saw Kareem play Wilt one day, it was just amazing," he said—and now, with the league at the height of its popularity, Nunn himself was a member of an elite team in the Pro division called the Courtsmen.

Coached by park legend Teddy Jones, Nunn teamed on the Courtsmen with Charlie Criss of New Mexico State, a five eight guard who, like Harthorne Wingo and so many others, parlayed the exposure and success he found at the Rucker tourney into an NBA career with Atlanta, Milwaukee, and San Diego.

The Courtsmen, who had won back-to-back Rucker championships under Jones in the summers of 1965 and 1966, were still among the elite teams at Rucker Park in the early '70s, though Julius Erving's Daily News All-Stars, coached by Pete Vecsey and Butch Purcell, were clearly at the top of the asphalt heap.

Other loaded teams always in contention for the coveted championship trophy were Hammond and Kirkland's Milbank squad; Small's Paradise, coached by Junior Martin; the Rucker Pros, coached by Carl Green; and Tiny Archibald's Bronx All-Stars, coached by Floyd Layne.

"It was an honor to play with and against such great players," said Nunn. "It was also a great ethnic melting pot in Harlem."

"White people were usually very leery about going up in that neighborhood," said Nunn, who was born to an Italian mother and African-American father. "But when it came to Rucker games, they felt comfortable driving or taking the train up there."

Nunn remembers white fans at Rucker Park sitting peacefully and side-by-side with black militant leaders like Stokely Carmichael and H. Rap Brown. They were huge public figures at that time. Sitting in the stands at Rucker Park, Carmichael and Brown had put down their political agendas to pick up the action that everyone in their community, and beyond, was talking about. "They just sat there," Nunn said, "like two ordinary basketball fans."

Nunn was no stranger to the great Dr. J., having played against Erving collegiately in 1971, a UMass–GW contest held at Madison Square Garden best remembered by a 36-point eruption from Walt Szczerbiak.

"I knew Erving was a pretty good basketball player from the time our two teams met in college," Nunn said. "But when I saw him at the Rucker, this guy was playing at another level, scoring fifty points a game against great competition like it was no big deal. The guy was just phenomenal."

A solid player, but one who was clearly not in the same league as an Erving or a Hammond, Nunn soon began to give up the dream of playing pro ball and decided to pursue other options.

While looking for another job, Nunn kept himself in basketball shape by joining a team in the Pro-Am League. Run by a man named Cecil Watkins, the Pro-Am staged its games at Hunter College in Manhattan and Roberto Clemente State Park in the Bronx. Watkins, one of college basketball's premier black referees in the 1960s, received his initial training officiating games at Rucker Park.

"Holcombe Rucker and I were great friends," said Watkins. "He couldn't always afford to pay people to ref his games, so I did it for free."

Watkins's league was now the place where many Rucker stars were shining, keeping their fragile egos, knees, and ankles away from the dangerous asphalt.

After a game at Roberto Clemente Park, Watkins approached Nunn.

"What are you doing still playing?" he asked.

"Just trying to keep myself in shape," Nunn said.

"Why don't you ref?" Watkins asked him.

Eventually, Nunn took Watkins up on his offer.

Watkins, who was hired by the NBA in 1972 as an observer scout for referees and would later become assistant supervisor of NBA officials for the league, sent Nunn and a handful of aspiring refs up to Rucker Park to gain the kind of valuable experience he had gained years earlier at the park.

Nunn, along with Lee Jones, Hugh Evans, and Dick Bavaetta, four of the NBA's best-known referees in recent years, all got their early training working Rucker League games.

Looking back, Jones said that he too owed an awful lot of what he had become to what Holcombe Rucker had started.

"What I got from all of them, the great players, the crazy fans, the experience of working there, and the ability to pass along everything I had learned about officiating to younger, aspiring refs, was just amazing," he said. "I'll never forget all the showboating, all the flashiness. It's unfortunate we just don't have that caliber of play in New York City anymore."

The Unthinkable

By the middle of the 1970s, with New York City in the midst of a fiscal crisis, the unthinkable happened. In 1975 the Rucker Tournament was moved out of Harlem to the Brandeis High School gymnasium at 84th Street and Columbus Avenue. The pros were still attending, but Holcombe Rucker was probably spinning in his grave.

"Somewhere up in basketball heaven, Mr. Rucker must have been crying," Hammond said. "He must have thought he lost his baby."

If that were indeed the case, Rucker's tears stopped flowing in the summer of 1977, when the Harlem Professionals, having raised enough money to resurface the court and give the park and its surroundings a bit of a facelift, brought their tournament back to its rightful home. By that time, however, the risk of injury was becoming too great to chance for professional hoop stars whose salaries were beginning to climb into the upper six figures.

A few name players did remain, such as Lloyd World B. Free of the Philadelphia 76ers, Larry McNeil of Golden State, and James "Fly" Williams of Brooklyn, who had run with the Spirits of St. Louis of the ABA and was signed at the time by the Seattle SuperSonics.

Williams once set the NCAA scoring mark for freshmen, averaging 29.4 points per game at Austin Peay in 1973, a mark that stood until it was broken by Chris Jackson of Louisiana State University in the 1988–89 season. ("FLY IS OPEN, LET'S GO PEAY!!!" is one of the most memorable chants in the history of the pro, college, or schoolyard game.)

Before making a name for himself at Austin Peay, Fly just couldn't get a run up at Rucker Park. During his high school playing days, few people knew his name, as he had split a rather quiet high school career between James Madison in Brooklyn and Glen Springs Academy Prep in Elmira, New York.

"That's how big the Rucker Tournament was in those days," said Fly, a six five shooting guard from Brownsville, Brooklyn, whose nickname stood for the fly manner in which the man dressed, and the fly manner in which he dressed down opponents on the basketball court. "If you didn't have a name, or you didn't know someone who put in a good word for you, you weren't playing, period. No team wanted me until after I came back from college."

By the time Fly came back from Austin Peay, basketball fans throughout the country were indeed buzzing about his titanic game, and the legendary chant that followed him from court to court.

"When I launched from half-court, they went and took it out of the net," Fly said. "I had range, baby, range."

Not only was Fly good enough by that time to play in Rucker Park, but the ABA's Spirits of St. Louis came calling in the 1974–75 season.

"That team was a perfect fit for Fly," Pete Vecsey said. "It was wide-open basketball, about the closest thing you could possibly get to playground basketball at the professional level."

The kid who couldn't get a game in Willie Mays's old neighborhood was now a teammate on that St. Louis squad with professional stars like Moses Malone, Marvin Barnes, and Freddie Lewis.

"We all had a ball," Fly said. "Even little Bobby. He was right there in the middle of it."

(Little Bobby, of course, is Bob Costas, the Spirits' spirited play-by-play man who is now a giant at NBC.)

But for Fly, the ABA party ended after just one season with the Spirits, in which he averaged 9.4 points, 2.5 boards, and 2 assists per game. He bounced around from team to team but ended up playing the next three seasons overseas, two in Tel Aviv and another in Paris.

Every summer, Fly flew back to New York and Rucker Park, the crossroads of the basketball universe. "Me and my boys played ball everywhere, against anyone, all the time," Fly said. "Basketball, basketball, basketball. The basketball light never went out on our small little planet."

Fly first ran at Rucker with a Brooklyn squad named RK Records, and then helped put together FEZ, the best Brooklyn entry the league had seen since Jackie Jackson and company of Brooklyn USA were giving Wilt and his crew all kinds of fits back in the 1960s. FEZ got their name from a Muslim youth organization named Morris American, which sponsored the team despite the fact that none of the players were Muslims. A man named Joseph Jeffrey-El, who coached FEZ and became an agent for several of the players, simply named the team after the brimless felt hats with the long tassels worn by many of the Muslims from the Morris American organization and other groups around the city.

Joining Fly on the FEZ roster were future NBA scoring machine World B. Free, Greg Jackson, a six-foot guard who played with the New York Knicks and Phoenix Suns during the 1974–75 season; Ed Searcy, the six six former St. John's stud who spent a minute with the Boston Celtics in the '75–'76 season; and Mel Davis, the six eight forward who played for both the New York Knicks and New York Nets in the mid-1970s.

"We did everything in that park but win a championship," Fly said. "But winning a championship wasn't as important to me as going up there to showcase. I needed the rep, and up at the Ruck, I got it for sure."

Fly did indeed have a rep at Rucker. He was notorious for dropping 50 on some hopeless defender before walking off the court in midgame and moving on to the next contest in search of better competition.

"I think I had enough, and I know you had enough," Fly would tell his humiliated foes.

But when the great trash-talkers like Pee Wee Kirkland and Joe Hammond got in Fly's ear, the king of cool often melted down.

"That was my one weakness out there," Fly admits. "I'd let guys get into my head and I'd get frustrated, and it would throw my game off a bit."

When his playing days ended, Fly's life went south. He reverted to using and selling drugs on his hard Brooklyn streets. He served two separate jail terms totaling four years, and nearly lost his life to a shotgun wound in the back that cost him a lung and a kidney.

"I went through what a lot of inner-city kids went through," Fly said. "But I'm grateful I'm alive and able to do what I'm now doing."

Fly, now fifty, is the vice president of Reality Check Foundation, a youth organization in Brooklyn that uses basketball to help keep kids on the hardwood and off the mean streets.

"This was the kind of thing that Holcombe Rucker did for kids like me that helped pave a path," Fly said. "My playing minutes are up, so it's time for me to do the same, brother."

World B. versus Shake & Bake

Fly Williams's old buddy World B. Free comes to the Brooklyn youth organization some weekends to lend a shooting hand with the kids. The two friends often reminisce about the old days at Rucker Park. The one game that often comes up in their conversation took place on a sweltering day at Rucker Park in the summer of 1977. On that day, Frank "Shake & Bake" Streety, one of the legendary playground phenoms on the Milbank roster, crossed basketball paths with World B. Free, the scoring machine from the Philadelphia 76ers.

The flamboyant and outspoken NBA All-Star (who would legally change his first name from Lloyd to World because, he said, "I'm moving up in the world, so I thought I better do something to commemorate it") strutted into the park that day the way so many professional players had done before him.

"World just looked at me and said, 'I'm gonna get mine,' " Streety remembered.

"Bring it on," Shake & Bake shot back.

Though he had never played on an NBA team, anyone who knew anything about hoops in those days knew Frank Streety.

"You can't talk about the great players of that era," says Pee Wee Kirkland, "without talking about Shake and Bake."

The Shake & Bake label was pasted on Streety in honor of the herky-jerky moves that became the trademark of this six-foot point guard. He would twist opponents in defensive knots and spin them like tops on the asphalt until he was good and ready to blow past them for easy layups or rim-rocking dunks that few other players his size were capable of executing.

A high school all-American who led Westinghouse to back-to-back Public Schools Athletic League championships in the early 1960s, Streety, who was also a great defensive player, became a star at Broome College in Binghamton, New York, before taking his crowd-pleasing act at the junior college level to Division I's Murray State in Kentucky.

Along the way, Shake & Bake did battle with some of college basketball's most revered point guards, including Dean Meminger of Marquette, Walt Frazier of Southern Illinois, and Calvin Murphy of Niagara University.

"I did some of my best work on 'Downtown' Freddie Brown," said Streety, referring to the Southeastern Community College (Iowa) star who would become an NBA All-Star with the Seattle SuperSonics. "I think I had thirty-something on him. I just killed him."

By the time World B. Free arrived to mix it up with Shake & Bake, Streety had already performed around the world for three years with the very best of the Harlem Globetrotters, including Meadowlark Lemon and Curly Neal. At a professional crossroads in his life, Shake & Bake had declined an offer to join the Detroit Pistons in a preseason tryout camp in 1970, choosing instead to sign with the Globetrotters.

"Curly and I did most of the dribbling," said Streety, who is immortalized in the old Harlem Globetrotter cartoons. "I'll never forget the night we played Madison Square Garden. I really turned the building out that night."

Before he'd ever thought about trying to conquer the World, Streety's mug had even made a cover of *Sports Illustrated*. Shake & Bake shared that cover with Lew Alcindor (soon to be known as Kareem Abdul-Jabbar) for a story about college basketball dismissing the almighty dunk.

"They used Alcindor as the big guy who got a lot of dunks, and me as the little guy who got a lot of dunks," Streety said.

A little guy with a high opinion of his game, Shake & Bake flew into a rage one day after reading in a basketball magazine that World B. had racked up 40 on him when the two players met back in 1977.

"Forty points was an overexaggeration," Streety said. "I was one of the league's top defensive players, so there's no way that World B. Free, never in his whole lifetime, was going to get forty against Frank Shake & Bake Streety."

To the best of Streety's recollection, he outscored World B. that day 25–16.

"I shaked and baked him throughout the game," Streety said. "By the time I was finished with him, he was very embarrassed."

Much like the Hammond–Dr. J. duel, there are a number of versions regarding World versus Streety. James "Fly" Williams, a teammate of World B.'s when he locked horns with Streety that day, said that World B. shook Shake & Bake out of his slippers and made him look foolish in front of the Harlem faithful.

"Man, World B. murdered Shake & Bake that day," Williams said. "Streety couldn't do nothing with World. If Streety didn't have a layup, he was lost out there, because that was all he could really do. He didn't even belong on the same court as World."

Ernie Morris, the Rucker historian who is widely considered the most trusted source in these matters, said that World B. did not get 40 that day, "but did get twenty-something," and did get the best of Streety.

"Back in those days, World B. was stronger than the average guard," said Morris. "The guy had phenomenal range. I mean, this was a guy hitting half-court jumpers with accuracy, nothing but bombs. Shake played good that day, but World played great."

Pee Wee Kirkland also said that scoring 40 points on Shake & Bake, even if a player was as great as World B., was nearly impossible.

"Frank Streety was as great a defensive guard then as Gary Payton is today," said Kirkland. "Forty points? I don't think so."

Shake & Bake insists that like many other tales from the blacktop, his encounter with World B. has grown in time as tall as some of the tallest players.

"World B. had a strong upper body and he liked to push people around," Streety said. "But he was a selfish player whose main objective was not to play defense or help his teammates but just to score points, so all I really had to do was just concentrate on denying him the ball, and that really frustrated him a lot."

Streety, like Holcombe Rucker before him, carries a passion and spirit for working with young kids. For twelve years he served as a resident adviser at Covenant House in New York, helping to put the pieces of shattered young lives back together again. He and his wife, Michelle, left New York for Kissimmee, Florida, shortly after the terror attacks of September 11.

"My wife worked for the Port Authority, on the sixty-ninth floor of one of those towers," Streety said. "She just happened to miss work that day."

Now in his late fifties, Streety offers basketball instruction to young children attending hoop clinics in nearby Poinciana.

Years after a remarkable but terribly underrated career, Frank Streety finally shared with us the ingredients to his Shake & Bake recipe, a routine that left so many of his archrivals looking like pretzels in hi-top sneakers:

Use two full servings of between-the-legs dribbling.

Toss in one behind-the-back dribble, left to right.

Toss in one behind-the-back dribble, right to left.

A touch of head-bob.

A quick-dash of shuffling feet.

Add a large dose of hesitation dribble.

Sprinkle a smattering of crossover dribbles until your opponent is good and red in the face.

Spin 360 degrees once, twice, to make sure your opponent is completely cooked.

Stick a fork in your opponent; he's done.

"I used that very same recipe on World B.," Streety said. "I embarrassed hundreds of ballplayers in my day, and on that day I embarrassed World B. Free.

"When I was leaving the park," Shake & Bake said, "people were wondering why he was a pro, and I wasn't."

Return of The Destroyer

Despite the shortage of pros, thousands still flocked to the park that summer, and were treated to an added bonus when The Destroyer, now twenty-six, surfaced from a three-year absence to tear up the competition.

With each passing game that summer, Hammond's scoring totals rose like the scorching temperature: 29 points in his first game back, 36 the next, then 59, which broke the outdoor league record. By game four of The Destroyer's comeback, even the basketball was sweating. Pro scouts were back in the bleachers to watch him explode for 73 points in a single contest, a Rucker record that would still be standing had The Destroyer not come along later to break it himself.

Incredibly, Hammond's 73-point rampage had come at the expense of Mike Riordan, who had been voted by NBA coaches as one of the top defensive players in their league.

"One by one, NBA players would come to the park to try to shut Joe down, but no one could do it," said Howie Evans of the *Amsterdam News*. "Cazzie Russell went up there talking all this smack about how he was going to lock up Joe. Well, they met in a game and Joe had thirty on him at halftime and the crowd was going wild. By the end of the game, Joe had fifty-six points and Cazzie left the park real mad, and he never came back."

The Arrival of White Jesus

In the summer of 1978 the Rucker crowds were being entertained by the highest-jumping and hardest-dunking white boy in the history of New York City. His name was Billy Rieser, a six-foot-four-inch kid from East Harlem and Benjamin Franklin High School who wore long hair, a Led Zeppelin T-shirt, bell-bottom jeans, and a short-brimmed black fedora. He carried a cane wherever he went, which put smiles on the faces of wiseguys who sat in front of social clubs on Pleasant Avenue, an old Italian neighborhood that stretches six blocks along the East River.

Rieser had a forty-four-inch vertical leap and potential that stretched much higher. In fact, he was coach Stan Dinner's first big-time recruit at Benjamin Franklin High School, the player who would help Franklin begin its return to schoolboy prominence.

Rieser had played his first two years of high school ball at my alma mater, St. Agnes, a small Catholic school in midtown Manhattan. The Stags, a little-known, Division III program in the Catholic High School Athletic Association, were barely a blip on the city's highly touted high school basketball radar screen.

But by the summer of 1976, word in Harlem began to spread about the fifteen-year-old Rieser, who was already squaring off and holding his own against Rucker playground legends like Joe Hammond, Helicopter Knowings, and Earl Manigault.

Most of those older legends had seen Rieser spread his wings above the outdoor courts at Jefferson Park on 114th Street and Pleasant Avenue, the place where he and I were both raised, and at the nearby La Guardia Memorial House on East 116th Street, where a number of major hoop tournaments were held year-round. Two years later he was a star at Rucker Park, where white players were now a thing of the past.

"I was just a kid, playing against these grown-up guys," said Rieser, who is now forty-two years old and living in Kentucky. "But ever since I could remember, I was dunking on guys, and I mean dunking hard.

"People weren't used to seeing that, especially from a white kid like me, especially in a neighborhood like East Harlem," he said. "Back then, it was very embarrassing to not only get dunked on, but to get dunked on severely."

Those severely embarrassing dunks at the La Guardia House often resulted in metal folding chairs being thrown onto the court in Rieser's direction by angry black fans who did not like what they were seeing and could barely believe it either.

But Billy Rieser just kept dunking. "I can't tell you how many nights I came home with bloody wrists," he said.

As Rieser's stock soared that summer, neighborhood folk, teammates, opposing players, and the many fans who had flocked to see his almighty game began calling him "White Jesus." Like Earl Monroe before him, Rieser's nickname was a tribute to his miraculous game.

"I'll never forget how The Goat pulled me aside one day after I had a real great game in the park," Rieser said. "He was high, I mean sky-high, and yet, he took the time to say to me, 'Young fella, you are going to be a great, great college player one day, a great Olympian, and a great pro. Just keep doing what you're doing.' "

Before long, Dinner and a number of his cohorts began preaching the word of big-time hoops to White Jesus.

"They told me that I was wasting my time at St. Agnes, that there was no exposure for me there," Rieser said. "And you know something? They were right."

So White Jesus tore up his train pass and transferred to Franklin. He left a predominantly white, all-boys school of about four hundred students, many of whom were the sons of foreign diplomats from the nearby United Nations, with a fine academic reputation, for Franklin, a predominantly black school of about twenty-five hundred students, many of them the worst the city had to offer.

"Me and Matty Cappuccilli, a guy I played with at Franklin, were among four white students in the whole school," Rieser said. "When I first got there, I was threatened at knifepoint and gunpoint, and I can't tell you how many guys I laid out in those hallways just to help keep myself alive." But that was before they were bowing to White Jesus, who patterned his open-floor attack after the games of Pistol Pete Maravich and three Rucker Park alums—Connie Hawkins, Julius Erving, and Walt Frazier.

"As soon as they came to the games and saw what I could do," Rieser said, "every kid in that school was cool with me."

They had seen White Jesus work miracles against PSAL powers like Taft High School, a game in which he took the ball off the opening tip, stormed upcourt, leaped from the foul line and threw a nasty two-handed dunk over the dome of a Taft player some four inches taller, a jam that ignited a twenty-minute jam-fest of fans who spilled out of their seats and onto the court in celebration.

"Everyone who knew me, knew I never dunked unless I had someone to dunk on," Rieser said. "Anyone can dunk if no one is guarding them, so if I was alone under the basket, I'd just lay it in, because every dunk has to have a purpose."

There were other legendary moments on the hardwood and in places like Rucker Park, like the time White Jesus outrebounded his PSAL rival, the great Sidney Green, during a regular season clash between Benjamin Franklin and Boys High at St. John's University in 1978. That same year, Rieser pinned New York Knick Dick Barnett on one end, then reverse-jammed him on the other during a pickup game at East 20th Street in Manhattan. And again that year, in his only game at Madison Square Garden, Rieser finished a perfect afternoon with 36 points and a combined, zero-missed shots from the field and free throw line against Morris High School of the Bronx.

"That game at the Garden, I'll never forget it," he said. "There's only one other time in my life when I felt that kind of magic, that kind of history and tradition when I stepped onto a basketball court.

"That was the court at Rucker Park," White Jesus said. "The people there really loved seeing me fly."

As his college playing days approached, Rieser had ignored recruitment interest from basketball powers like St. John's, North Carolina, Notre Dame, Purdue, Louisville, and UCLA, and, swayed by the monetary powers of boosters from the South, landed at Centenary College in Shreveport, Louisiana. A Shreveport oil baron took a liking to the white kid from Harlem, filled his pockets with some dollars and his mind with some bull, then gave him a new Cutlass to seal the deal.

Things were actually going pretty well for White Jesus at Centenary. He was averaging 16 points per game and raising Southern eyebrows with the explosive air show that had made him a celebrity in the old neighborhood. After each game, the oil baron would leave a stack of cash under the mat in the Cutlass. The amount of money in that stack was always in proportion to the amount of points, assists, and rebounds that White Jesus put on the stat sheet that night. Special crowd-pleasing slams usually translated into special bonuses.

In March 1994, White Jesus told the *New York Daily News*'s Mark Kriegel about the oil baron's heftiest bonus, which came after a spectacular dunk against Northeast Louisiana, a team that featured Calvin Natt and his brother Kenny.

"It was our last home game," White Jesus said. "I took the ball on the fly off a full-speed run, then two quick steps and a perfect jump. I cocked it and took off right inside the foul line. I never threw it so hard on anyone as I threw it then on Kenny Natt. The perfect dunk. It left a bruise on my wrist. You know it was a nasty one when you break the skin. But this one was real nasty. I came down with a scowl, like I wanted to kill someone. Like I said, I was invincible."

But that aura of invincibility disappeared a week before Rieser's sophomore season, when he blew out a knee playing pickup ball.

"They didn't scope you back then, they cut you," he said. "The operation was November 3. By January 3, I'm playing in my first game. I couldn't move. I'm no good at all. By the seventh game, I tell the coach, 'My knee's still bad. I gotta go.' He says, 'Fine, just leave your sneakers.' "

Billy Rieser (aka White Jesus), elevating
(*Centenary College, Shreveport, Louisiana*)

That evening just happened to be Billy Rieser Poster Night, with fans waving placards of Rieser's memorable dunk on Kenny Natt.

"Billy left his sneakers at the locker room door," Kriegel wrote. "All of a sudden, White Jesus was just another hard-luck kid a long way from Harlem."

After two failed seasons at Eastern Kentucky, Rieser came home. His wings severely clipped down South, White Jesus had enough left to form an alliance at Rucker Park with "Sudden" Sam Worthen, a six six point guard from Franklin Lane in Brooklyn who played as an all-American for Al McGuire at Marquette before joining the Chicago Bulls, and a fancy six two guard named Dancing Doogie on the KISS FM All-Stars.

"High-jumping Billy," said Sudden Sam, a smile joining hands with a memory. "He never backed down from anybody on a basketball court, and even with a bad knee, he was skying out there and slamming on people."

Indeed, White Jesus proved to large, mostly black audiences that the white man who had sold his soul to the oil baron could still jump.

"That was such a fun time for me because I was home, in front of people who knew me, in front of people who liked me just for me," he said. "What made it even more special was the fact that I was still good enough to play at Rucker Park. Every neighborhood has its courts, and everyone who plays serious basketball has his court. My court was in Jefferson Park. I owned that court from sunrise to sunset.

"But Rucker Park," White Jesus said. "It has the single most, best reputation of any park in America. It is the place where ordinary games turn into extraordinary games through some aura, some magic in the atmosphere."

White Jesus played that entire season, thrilling fans with a dunk he had perfected in college: "I would stand on one side of the rim and have somebody lob me a pass from in front of the bench, on the other side of the rim. Once the ball went over the rim, I leaped, turned my body away from the rim, caught it, double-pumped in midair, then threw it down backward."

Before long, the Rucker was crawling with scouts, and White Jesus got offers to play professionally in Venezuela and France.

But his knees started creaking again, and his back and his ankles began screaming louder and louder with each passing dribble, each passing dunk.

"I was always able to do whatever I wanted on a basketball court. I was a good, all-around fundamental player," he said. "But when all the injuries started mounting, it affected me mentally, and if I couldn't dominate a basketball game anymore, I just didn't want to be around it."

Eventually Rieser moved his family to Kentucky, where he now runs a telecommunications company. He also plays lots of golf, reads the Bible frequently, and makes the time in his community "to preach the word of the Lord."

Twenty years later, White Jesus may have found God and lost his almighty hops, but he still finds time to reminisce and laugh about the old days, about the old neighborhood, about Benjamin Franklin, Stan Dinner, and the oil baron, and about Rucker Park and his famous dunks.

"I had a game that was a little bit different from what people might have expected from a guy who looked like I did," he said.

"You couldn't learn to jump like I could jump in any classroom," said White Jesus, staring to the heavens as he spoke. "That was a gift that came from God."

End of an Era

By the turn of the decade, NBA salaries had continued getting stupid, and the players smarter, taking the advice of their agents and keeping their knees and ankles away from the parks. In the summer of '80, the arrival of pro stars at Rucker Park had slowed to a trickle, with an occasional visit from a Louis Orr, a Pat Cummings, or a Sam Worthen. Even the top playground stars had disappeared from the schoolyard landscape. Hammond was in and out of prison on drug-related charges, though he did make one last, dramatic cameo, breaking his own single-season scoring record between trips to Rikers Island with a 76-point outburst playing for a team called Coca-Cola, which also included former NBA players Ed Searcy and Larry McNeill, famous for winning the NBA's first slam-dunk contest.

Kirkland, who had stormed out of the Chicago Bulls' training camp after a squabble over playing time, was also behind bars, serving time for tax evasion and an assortment of other crimes.

The Rucker community had already suffered another crushing blow that spring, when Harlem's Helicopter man, Herman Knowings, was killed in a car accident on April 12. Holcombe Rucker's son, Phil, who had taken the reins of his father's tournament two years earlier, held a benefit game in honor of the Helicopter that included two of his former Globetrotter teammates, Pablo Robertson and Bobby Hunter.

Everyone at the benefit game recalled the man from South Carolina, whose flights to the hoop in New York City were measured the way football statisticians measure punts—in hangtime.

"I thought I was this big star from Seward Park High," Hunter said. "But this guy started to bend my fingers back, blocking every shot of mine. Next game I got him on my side."

One Helicopter tale that hovers above the rest took place at a Rucker League game, when Helicopter went airborne in the paint to block an opponent's shot. But the opponent decided to fake the shot, holding onto the ball and not about to release it until the Helicopter came back down to earth. The only problem was that the Helicopter stayed airborne in his defensive position. The opponent got so confused, he just held onto the ball and was called for a three-second violation.

"Copter could really fly," Hammond said. "It's a damn shame he had to die like that. He wasn't like me and the rest of the guys who went running around the streets. Copter was totally legit, and look what happened."

Chapter 6

RETURN OF THE GOAT

I n the summer of 1980, Earl Manigault returned to his domain and brought back the Goat Tournament.

"When I was growing up, I looked up to guys like Tom Sanders, Cal Ramsay, and Holcombe Rucker," Manigault said. "The kids I left behind looked up to me. They needed me to come back."

Kareem Abdul-Jabbar understood Manigault's desire to return to the streets of their old neighborhood. "He represents a lot to that community," Abdul-Jabbar said. "He represents a failure where there could have been achievement. A lot of the people there live with a certain sense of failure, so they can relate to him."

More important, Manigault had finally managed to kick his drug habit for good.

"It was killing my body, and I was tired of looking the same way day in and day out," Manigault explained. "It took a lot of guts and a lot of pain, but I did it. I came out of it the way I went into it. No medication, no hospitals, no counseling."

Though Manigault had won the war against drugs, too many earlier lost battles with alcohol, marijuana, cocaine, and heroin had left him frail, soft-spoken, and weak.

The Goat was dying, and so too was the arena that helped

make the Goat a household name throughout Harlem and basketball points beyond.

In fact, the last of a long, prominent line of pros were dancing on the Pied Piper's magnificent stage, performing for Pete Vecsey and Butch Purcell on the last of their great Westsider teams in the early 1980s.

"Sudden" Sam Worthen of the Chicago Bulls, Pat Cummings of the Milwaukee Bucks, and Louis Orr of Indiana were the final stars on a Westsiders squad once headlined by Julius Erving and Charlie Scott.

"We won the last real Rucker Championships," said Worthen. "We were the last real pro team in that park."

Worthen, who would score the first two points in USBL history as a member of the Springfield Fame in 1985, and later become the first man to play and coach in that semipro league that has served as a springboard for developing players who often leap to the NBA, won another championship during Rucker Park's early transition years with Pookie Wilson and the Chic All-Stars in 1985. That squad also included Steve "All Day" Burtt of Iona fame and Kevin Williams, the ex–St. John's star who played the point for five different NBA teams from 1983 to 1989.

Sudden Sam, his nickname coined by Al McGuire, had a penchant for whipping sudden, no-look, on-the-money passes from anywhere and everywhere to teammates when motoring down the lane. Sudden Sam began wowing Rucker Park crowds even before his days at Marquette, back when he teamed with future Detroit Pistons badboy Vinnie "Microwave" Johnson at McLennan Junior College in Waco, Texas.

"Everywhere I went, people asked me about the Rucker Tournament," Worthen said. "Coach McGuire, he loved the Rucker,

and he loved going up there to watch the games. Every time the
two of us sat down to talk basketball, Rucker Park always came
up. We always talked about how every time you went up there,
you always saw something different, something unexpected, but
that whatever it was, it was always exciting."

Worthen, who also played and coached with the Harlem Wizards and is an assistant coach with the Fayetteville Patriots of
the NBA's Development League, credits nearly every word on his
basketball résumé to his days in Rucker.

"Playing at Rucker early in my career prepared me to handle
pressure situations in front of big crowds," said Sudden Sam.
"By the time I got to college and the pros, I wasn't intimidated
by all those screaming people, and that really helped me, especially during games on the road."

Sudden Sam said that the pro versus playground rivalry was still
going strong during the Westsiders' last years of existence. "We
didn't have a Joe Hammond to deal with, but we had playground
legends like Pookie Wilson, Richie Adams, and The Terminator,
Ronnie Mathias," he said. "Those guys gave us fits out there."

Sudden Sam suddenly became somber. "You know, all those
pros not coming out there anymore—it's a real loss for the fan,"
he said. "Think about it, you had NBA All-Stars out there playing for free, for free!

"Those days," he said softly, "are gone forever."

New Show in Town

The "real" Rucker days that Sudden Sam spoke of were now in
the park's rearview mirror. By the summer of 1982, the Rucker
Tournament's wobbly legs were about to give out. Pro stars had

disappeared, and the top high school and collegiate players were doing their thing elsewhere.

Sensing a need to shift the tournament's emphasis from steak to sizzle, a rapper and Harlem native named Greg Marius created a flaky but equally entertaining cousin of the Rucker Tourney called the Entertainers Basketball Classic, and moved the games to Mount Morris Park.

Before creating the EBC, Marius was a member of a rap group called the Disco Four. The group loved playing basketball as much as they loved rapping, which planted the seeds for the new league.

"The EBC started with us, the Disco Four, playing against the Crash Crew," said Al Cash, deejay of the Disco Four who now serves as one of the main announcers at EBC games. "Then Grandmaster Flash & The Furious 5 and other rappers challenged us. We started out as entertainers and then picked up real street ballplayers such as Walter Berry, Pearl Washington, Olden Polynice, Richie Adams, and Kenny Hutchinson. Those cats are really pioneers of the Entertainers Basketball Classic."

The EBC's trademark would be a run-and-gun style of play in which players would be judged not so much by winning but by the individual moves they brought to entertain the crowds. Almost everyone got a nickname, even those players who didn't deserve one, and the play-by-play was now done by men who were half Marv Albert, half Jay-Z, barking their color commentary and wisecracks from microphones while a hip-hop soundtrack played hard and loud from courtside.

"There goes the Shuttleman, wandering around out there like he's lost in Times Square and can't find his way to Grand Central Station," was one of the classic early calls of the legendary

Duke "Tango" Mills, who still works the microphone at EBC games.

Marius was determined to keep Holcombe Rucker's spirit alive, so he dialed up some of his buddies from the overlapping worlds of showbiz and basketball to help create his new league. The players as a whole were not quite as spectacular as they once were, so Marius pumped a little more energy into the carnival-like atmosphere, a little more hoopla into his version of hoops.

That explains the presence of Duke, a forty-something, quick-talking, quicker-witted wisecracker and deejay/play-by-play man who calls it as only he sees it.

When all that noise from the stone bleachers begins to fade, all in attendance have their eyes fixed on Duke, who is ready to offer his own version of the national anthem.

Duke clears his throat: "You're with me, I'm with you. We are all together as one. United we stand. Divided we fall. Now let's play ball!"

The crowd roars. They toss up the rock. It's showtime. . . .

"Afro Puffs rises for a jump shot, but Long Fingers gets a piece of it," says Duke, working the crowd like a nightclub co-median. "Here they come the other way. The Handler makes his way through traffic and feeds the Undertaker, who buries an-other one."

Duke is now joined behind the mike by three of his play-by-play associates: Al Cash, one half of the broacast duo of Tango and Cash; Boobie Smooth, aka "The Politician"; and a lovable crowd favorite named Honorable Hannibal, who strolls the side-lines with mike in hand and a World Wrestling Federation championship belt draped over one shoulder. The Honorable one is still defending a title he never owned.

"My favorite player is the Predator, because of the way he goes about stalking his prey on the basketball court," the great Hannibal once said. "This guy goes about six six and 270 pounds. I've admired this guy for years, and we're real good friends. You know, now that I think about it, I never stopped to ask him for his real name, but it really doesn't matter, does it?"

These four emcees are as legendary in Rucker Park as the very legends they've given nicknames to. The tags are straight out of World Wrestling Entertainment: Black Widow, Skip-To-My-Lou, Future, Best-Kept-Secret, 9-1-1, the Answer, the Master, the Undertaker, and perhaps the greatest Rucker Park nickname of all time: Half-Man, Half-Amazing.

"If I give you a nickname, that's the nickname you have for life," says Duke. "I love to work the crowd, I love when it gets off the hook up there. There's no other job like it in the world. When I'm describing the action, I know what to say, when to say it, and how to say it."

The crowd loves the Duke, and so do the players. Well, maybe not those players who are coming off the bench.

"Ladies and gentlemen," says the Duke, "it's SCRUBstitution time!"

And just how does the Duke come up with all of those clever nicknames?

"I usually go by their style of play," he says. "The first time I saw Kareem Reid play, none of us really knew how good he was, so I started calling him the Best-Kept-Secret.

"Rafer Alston, he just kind of skips by you when he dribbles, so I named him Skip-To-My-Lou. David Cain, I love the way he directs the offense, so I call him The Director."

One of Duke's classic nicknames was given to a playground

phenom named Malloy Nesmith, aka The Future. "I'm telling
you, this kid was making moves that weren't supposed to be invented for the next twenty years," explains Duke. "He was way
ahead of his time."

To the Duke, Joe Smith of the Golden State Warriors will always be 9-1-1, the Emergency Man. "Joe played in one game,
and he showed up late, in an emergency. I looked across the
street while he was playing and saw an ambulance. I said to myself, 'I have to call this guy the Emergency Man, or better yet,
9-1-1.' "

Physically and financially drained after financing the new
league out of his own pocket, Greg Marius did not organize a
tournament in 1984, snapping a thirty-eight-year run of summer
tourneys started by Rucker.

The Pied Piper's house was empty, but Rucker Park alums
were everywhere.

By 1986, Marius was completely reenergized. The tournament was back, and Marius even used his entertainment con-
nections to lure then NBA slam-dunk champ Dominique
Wilkins to the park to judge the EBC's very own throwdown
jamfest.

In 1987, Marius brought Holcombe Rucker's baby back to its
rightful crib at 155th Street and Eighth Avenue. Though it was
back on hallowed ground, the Rucker Tournament that had
helped hundreds of players get on separate paths to college ball
and the NBA was now on life support. The fans continued to
show up, but the caliber of competition was not very good. The
league had no sponsors, and more often than not, players would
run up and down the court during tournament games wearing
different jerseys.

With the games now played in a hip-hop environment, however, there was hope ahead, as Marius's league now had a unique platform that would offer sponsors and advertisers a stellar opportunity to reach large, young audiences that enjoyed basketball and music.

The Show Goes On

While Marius and a new band of players were inheriting the Pied Piper's grand old stage, Holcome Rucker's most electrifying cast member was making a name for himself at the Clinton Penitentiary in Dannemora, New York.

It has been said, in fact, that in the long, hard history of Dannemora, no two inmates were more famous than the notorious gangster Charles "Lucky" Luciano and Harlem's Destroyer, Joe Hammond.

"An older, high-ranking officer at Dannemora told me that when Lucky was in there, they built him a church," Hammond said. "For me, they built a basketball league."

From 1985 to 1988, Hammond split hard time for conspiracy to sell drugs between the Camp Gabriels Prison in Lake Placid and Dannemora.

"I damn near froze to death in Lake Placid," he said. "It got so cold up there, your spit turned to ice before it ever hit the ground."

During the time Hammond spent at Lucky Luciano's alma mater, prison officials, well aware of who Hammond once was, met his request to organize a basketball league.

"I told them it would do those guys in there some good," Hammond said. "They needed something in their lives to get their minds off all the violence that was going on behind them bars."

When prison officials signed off on the new league, one of them said to Hammond: "If there is any fighting, or stabbing, or any kind of trouble in any of these games, the league will be eliminated, and you will be held personally responsible."

Three weeks later the same prison official approached The Destroyer.

"It's unbelievable," he told him. "This is a maximum security prison, and by forming a league in here, you turned this place into a community center."

Before long, Hammond was doing his thing before large crowds in the prison courtyard, as inmates and prison guards sat side-by-side, high-fiving each other after spectacular moves put on by The Destroyer.

The familiar chants of "We want Joe, we want Joe" filled the yard the way they once filled Rucker Park, when Joe Hammond was a somebody, on his way to somewhere.

With nothing but spare time on his hands, Hammond devised a scheme to hustle money, food, and favors from the good citizens of the Clinton Penitentiary.

"I started holding free throw shooting competitions," said The Destroyer. "I would take on inmates, guards, visitors, all comers—but I wasn't going to compete unless there was something to compete for."

Hammond, who earned money doing odd jobs around the prison, usually put up small cash or cartons of cigarettes, even his sneakers, against the wagers that poured in from his fellow inmates. Those inmates who had little money would put up cans of tuna fish they had stolen from the prison commissary or from their comrades in stripes. On paydays, prison guards would set up their own little one-on-ones with The Destroyer.

"They knew how good a player I was at that time," said Hammond, referring to the guards and his fellow inmates. "But everyone wanted the bragging rights that came with beating me."

But The Destroyer never lost. At one point the man whom Howie Evans had never seen miss a free throw hit 93 in a row from the charity stripe.

"Number ninety-four rattled in and out," Hammond said. "Goddamn bumblebee started buzzing right around my eyes."

Before Joe Hammond was released from Dannemora in 1988, almost everyone associated with the facility owned his autograph, and he owned at least one thing or another that had once belonged to them.

"I'll never forget the day they opened my cell to tell me I was a free man," Hammond said. "One of the guards saw a sheet covering a large pile in the corner of my cell."

One guard grabbed Hammond; the other drew his gun and slowly walked toward the pile. He whipped off the cover and found more than five hundred cans of tuna fish The Destroyer had been storing in his cell.

"They never said a word, because everyone knew how I got that tuna," Hammond said. "They asked me if I wanted to take it home, and I just said, 'Nah, you guys eat it. I've had tuna for dinner every night this whole year.'"

A Familiar Face

After Joe Hammond's prison stint at Dannemora, he returned to his Harlem roots and his bad habits. Running again with the wrong crowd, he got hooked on cocaine and spent far too many nights drifting from crack den to crack den.

Then one night in the winter of 1990, under the lamplight of an East Harlem street, a familiar face returned. A group of neighborhood kids were playing touch football, their game interrupted on occasion by slow walking pedestrians and passing cars. On the sidewalk, two friends and I stood clustered in the doorway of an abandoned building, chatting, watching the game, and hiding from a howling October wind.

During the game, a man hobbled out of the shadows of a nearby alley. He appeared to be wandering aimlessly, but found his way onto the cement playing field.

"Yo, get your bum self off the field," said one of the boys. "We're playing a game."

The stranger, wearing a baseball cap and dressed in a baggy sweatshirt that he wore inside out and a pair of tattered blue jeans, continued on his course, forcing the game to a halt.

"Yo, my man, you deaf or something?" asked another boy.

It wasn't until the man stepped directly beneath the lamplight that he came into focus—a light-skinned black man with a short beard, middle-aged, tall and slender. He was clutching a brown paper bag in his large hands.

"I got address books and greeting cards I'm trying to sell," he told the group of angry boys. "I'm just trying to get something to eat."

Before things got out of hand, I rushed from the doorway and out onto the street. The boys, anticipating a fight, stepped back. We stood face-to-face, and as the stranger repeated his sales pitch, my eyes grew wide in disbelief.

"Joe Hammond, The Destroyer?" I asked. "Is that you?"

"Yeah, it's me, man. It's me."

Joe Hammond in 1991 *(New York Times)*

Like everyone else who grew up in Harlem, I knew everything there was to know about the legend of Joe Hammond. I had seen him play late in his magnificent career in 1977 at the La Guardia House, a community center on East 116th Street where The Destroyer's name still hangs on a golden, wall-of-fame plaque. I had seen quick glimpses of him in the old neighborhood in the late 1970s, when he traveled with an entourage as big as Muhammad Ali's.

The Destroyer was as well known to me as any of the sports

heroes I'd idolized as a kid. "It's been a long time," I said to Hammond. "How've you been?"

"I've seen better days," he said. "Right now I'm just trying to get me something to eat."

The neighborhood boys watched as the two of us spoke for a short while. I thanked The Destroyer for the memories and gave him some money. I told him that one day, I'd love to write a story about him.

"If you're from here, around the East Side, you can call me anytime," Hammond said to me. "I always take care of my people."

We shook hands. And then Hammond, still clutching his paper bag, disappeared into the night.

"I had to get out of there," he told me a short time later. "It hurts to have the people I know see me this way. This is not the way I want them to remember me. To most of them, I'm still a legend."

At that time, Hammond was living in an East Harlem housing project with his childhood sweetheart, Beverly Seabrook, and their sixteen-year-old daughter, Joy. (Hammond, who has never married, has four children from three separate relationships.)

Seabrook, who met Hammond at P.S. 45 on East 120th Street when the two were teenagers, was sitting in her apartment one day with an old scrapbook, the pages filled with newspaper clippings and photos of Hammond.

"I was the homecoming queen of my school, and he was this big basketball star everyone used to make such a fuss over," Seabrook said. "It doesn't seem so long ago that people were treating Joe like a king. For the two of us, I thought it would all work out like a fairy tale."

The king and the queen were still together, but the fairy tale was long over. "You tell me," said Hammond, shaking his head in disgust that day we met. "Is that the stuff that legends are made of?"

The Animal

Like Joe Hammond before him, Richie "The Animal" Adams was another Rucker Park alum about to make the journey from playing time to jailtime.

Adams, a troubled star from Benjamin Franklin High School in East Harlem, was recruited by Las Vegas coach Jerry Tarkanian. At the University of Nevada–Las Vegas, where the Animal played from 1981 to 1982 and again from 1983 to 1985, problems from an undisciplined childhood in New York plagued him. He missed home, missed hanging out with what he called his "get-high" buddies, and began using drugs more frequently.

"I was a hoodlum. I missed running in the streets," Adams said. "I began using marijuana and cocaine. At times during practice, I would just go into a corner all by myself and not talk to anyone. They started calling me a manic depressive, and they even sent me to a psychiatrist."

After his first season at UNLV, Adams went back to the South Bronx, where he had grown up, and again ran into trouble. "Whenever he went home, it was always something," Tarkanian said. "We knew we'd get a call about one thing or another."

Begged by Tarkanian to return to school, Adams went back to Las Vegas. But he had missed too many classes and was forced to sit out the season as a redshirt.

In each of his last two seasons at UNLV, Adams said, he sulked and continued to use drugs.

Despite his admitted drug abuse, Adams continued to excel on the court. In each of his last two seasons, in which the Rebels finished with a combined record of 57–10, he was selected the Pacific Coast Athletic Association Player of the Year. He finished at UNLV with 1,168 points and 623 rebounds.

"He had unlimited talent," said Tarkanian, who compared him as a player to Larry Johnson, who recently retired from a long and fairly productive NBA career. "He had that kind of ability. He could play tough, really rebound. And he had a nice turn-around jump shot."

Considered a legitimate professional prospect, Adams played on summer nights at Rucker Park, where his superb instincts for roundball caught the eye of a visiting scout with the Long Island Knights of the United States Basketball League. It wasn't long before NBA scouts decided that Adams was good enough to be a player in their league.

In June 1985 he was drafted by the Washington Bullets, the eighty-first pick in the fourth round. But on the same day he was drafted by the Bullets, Adams was arrested for stealing a car. The charges were eventually dropped, but the Animal continued to defy authority. He began breaking curfew in Bullets' camp and climbing out of hotel windows in the middle of the night to find a place where he could party.

Eventually, inevitably, he was cut.

After a two-year stint with a club team in Argentina, Adams returned to New York, settling in the Bronx. He had two young children from two separate relationships to support, no job, and, outside of putting a basketball through a hoop, no skills.

By 1991, the man who once wore No. 31 as a star player for the Runnin' Rebels was wearing No. 89T2957 on the green jacket that was part of his uniform at the Bare Hill Correctional Facility, a medium security prison tucked away in the Adirondacks, where I visited him in March of that year.

The Animal, now twenty-eight and serving four and a half to nine years for first-degree robbery and two counts of fourth-degree grand larceny, had wasted his God-given talents.

Instead of signing autographs at NBA games, he was practicing ten- to twelve-foot jump shots in the prison courtyard, his spirits, like his beat-up leather basketball, nearly deflated.

"This was the same guy I once saw school Patrick Ewing in college, when Ewing was at Georgetown," Billy Rieser said. "I mean, he rocked Patrick's world, snuffed his stuff on almost

Richie Adams at the Bare Hill Correctional Facility, Malone, New York *(Paul O. Boisvert)*

every play. Go check the tape of that game if you don't believe me.

"The point is," Rieser said, "this was a guy who belonged in the NBA, not prison."

Instead, here was the Animal, left to think, twenty-four hours a day, about all the wrong turns he had made.

"I can't believe this has happened to me," Adams said to me that day as a pair of shotgun-toting prison guards watched our little one-on-one. "Sometimes I hate myself for all the good things in life that I let slip away. I've been punished, and it's hard to deal with."

For the next three years the Animal called my home, collect, on a nightly basis, to talk to me and to be patched in with his network of friends.

Finally the Animal was paroled in 1994. He moved in with an old girlfriend on Manhattan Avenue and joined a team in Rucker Park called the X-Men, which was led by former St. John's stars David "The Director" Cain and Lamont Middleton, and former Manhattan Center and LIU standout Richie Parker.

With Adams in the middle of the action, the X-Men won a pair of championships in the mid-1990s, as no team could match the tenacity of the Animal in the low blocks. Not even the X-Men's fiercest rival, Flavor Unit, a guard-oriented team that featured some of the most recent backcourt hotshots on the playground scene: "Master" Rob Hockett, a former star at the University of New Orleans who spent a few seasons with the Harlem Globetrotters; Kerry "Natural Born Controller" Thompson, the ex–Florida State guard; and playground phenom James "Speedy" Williams.

"Obviously he wasn't the player he once was," said Cain, who came this close once to making Pat Riley's Knicks. "But you would see flashes of his brilliance on the court. Defensively, Richie was still an enforcer; he still had a presence in the paint. He still gave us that shot-blocking presence, and in spurts, whenever he swatted a guy's shot away or pinned a ball against the board or ripped a rebound and started a fast break, he looked like the Richie Adams all of us used to know."

On the court, at least in spurts, this was still the same Richie Adams who had wowed capacity crowds at Benjamin Franklin High School, UNLV, and Rucker Park throughout the years, the same player basketball experts once compared to the great Bill Russell.

In October 1996, trouble found Richie Adams again. This time he was arrested in connection with the murder of a teenage girl in the South Bronx. He was eventually found guilty of manslaughter but acquitted on a second-degree murder charge. His sentence carried a minimum of ten years and a maximum of twenty-five.

The verdict sent shock waves coast to coast.

"I love Richie," Jerry Tarkanian said. "But he just never made a right decision."

Closer to home, the people who came to know and love the Animal, including me, were heartbroken, and still in denial.

"It doesn't sound like Richie at all," Sidney Green said at the time. "I hope they find the right person, but Richie Adams? No way."

Lamont Middleton, his ex-teammate from those joyous X-Men days at Rucker Park who now works in athletics at St. John's, said, "I still don't believe it. Prison is not the kind of place for people like Richie Adams. He's not the kind of animal that some people think he is."

The Future Pros

By the end of the 1980s, an abundance of talent was once again filling Rucker Park, creating a number of intriguing matchups and story lines. Perhaps the best of games during the EBC's early years took place in August 1989, when a bunch of kiddie ballers calling themselves the Future Pros clashed with grizzled park veterans for the EBC Championship.

Though the Future Pros seemed far too young and inexperienced to make serious noise that summer, here they were, having made a Cinderella run through the regular season, and now they were preparing to jump it up against a polished and veteran team called Jay's All-Stars that was heavily favored to win the contest.

The Future Pros were led by The Future himself, Malloy Nesmith, a five eleven park magician from Jacksonville Junior College and later Utah State; Malik "The Freak" Sealy, who was taking his act from Tolentine High School in the Bronx to St. John's; Lamont Middleton of Walton High School in the Bronx, who was also on his way to St. John's; Carlton "Dunkin" Hines of the high school hoop power Manhattan Center; John "The Gladiator" Morton and Gordon Winchester, both Seton Hall bound; Chris Brooks of West Virginia fame; and Ernie Myers, who had played at Tolentine and was a key member of Jim Valvano's North Carolina State squad that stunned the basketball world in 1983, winning the NCAA championship on a last-second put-in by Lorenzo Charles.

Virtually unknown at the time, the Future Pros were going against players five to ten years older, several of them having already achieved professional status. Jay's All-Stars were captained by "Everyone's MVP," a gifted park rat from John Jay College named Pookie Wilson.

The rest of the cast included top-flight phenoms like Steve "All Day" Burtt, Iona's all-time leading scorer who had already had stints with the Golden State Warriors and Los Angeles Clippers; Troy "TNT" Truesdale, a six seven, 225-pound forward who teamed with Burtt at Iona and later played professionally overseas; and "Mr. Excitement," Darryl MacDonald, who played at Texas A&M before moving on to play professionally on foreign soil.

"They had a great, great team," The Future said, "but they didn't know how great we were until they walked off the court that day."

From the opening possession, The Future and Morton, teaming in the backcourt, were just too quick, too crafty, too cocky, too damn-everything for Jay's guard-tandem of Wilson and Burtt.

"The crowd was just buggin'," said Duke Tango Mills, who had the honor of doing play-by-play that evening. "They were like, 'Where the hell did these kids come from?'"

Midway through the first half of a close game, the high-rising Sealy snatched a rebound from out of the clouds, and before his rubber soles ever kissed asphalt, zipped a long over-the-shoulder pass to The Future, who had broken ahead of the field.

"I raced to the rim," The Future said, "and caught one helluva hard dunk."

With an ecstatic crowd smelling a possible upset, a pair of large brown pit bulls along the Jay's sideline began smelling the flesh of the two officials working the game.

A tough street hustler known only as Alpo, who had more

than a few Benjamins riding on the favorite, was unhappy with the way some of the calls had gone to that point in the contest. So Alpo loosened up a bit on both leashes during a timeout and shouted toward both refs while players from each team were huddled and talking strategy.

"Yo, refs," Alpo barked above the noise of the large crowd. "You mothers make one more bad call, and I'm gonna turn both your asses into dinner."

As Alpo spoke, he began walking slowly toward the officials. The closer Alpo got to the men in stripes, the louder his pit bulls growled, and a nervous crowd began to go silent. Finally there was just the sight of Alpo's hungry dogs at midcourt and the sounds of their loud, hungry growls. The atmosphere had suddenly turned from festive to frightening. Frozen with fear, both refs began backpedaling slowly.

"The whole crowd, and even the players, got real scared," The Future said. "Guys from both teams had to calm Alpo down. It took a while for us to convince him to get his dogs out of there."

When play resumed, the Future Pros continued to outclass the older, more experienced Jays. Morton was on his way to a 35-point performance, and The Future filled the stat sheet with 25 more, including numerous assists.

"We busted their butts," The Future said. "We was just kids, but we was on a mission."

When the final horn sounded on that dog-day afternoon, their mission was accomplished. The Future Pros held off a late rally by Jay's and hung on for a 86–83 upset victory. The Future and Morton, who had combined for 60 of those 86 points, were named co-MVPs.

"I still have that championship trophy. It's a lot taller than me," The Future said. "Every time I look at it, it brings back all those good memories of that game, of Carlton and Malik smiling.

"We was young," The Future said, "but we had the heart of a lion."

The Future Pros, who were together just for that one special season in Rucker Park, were aptly named. Sealy enjoyed an eight-year career in the NBA with Indiana, the Los Angeles Clippers, Detroit, and Minnesota before being killed in a car accident in May 2000. Morton played three years in the NBA with Cleveland and Miami from 1989 to 1992; Middleton played professionally in Australia and France, and Winchester played pro ball in Switzerland and Ireland. Hines, murdered at the age of twenty-two in 1994, never realized his dream of playing pro ball.

As for The Future, he never made it to the pros, but got as close as playing in Cecil Watkins's Pro-Am Tournament in the summer of 2001. The Future was the sixth man on a monster squad called Dyckman, which was headlined by NBA players like Anthony Mason, Rafer Alston, Mark Jackson, and fellow St. John's graduate Shawnelle Scott. The five eleven Nesmith averaged 18 points for that Dyckman squad, receiving roughly twenty-five minutes of playing time per game.

The Future's higher-profiled teammates knew he could hang with them at the next level. "Future," Jackson said, "definitely has the raw talent to become a pro."

One of Rucker Park's most famous players for three decades, The Future had begun to take his free-spirited game indoors in the hope that a Pat Riley or a Phil Jackson might wander into the gym one day and say "he's my man."

At New York's Hunter College, where the Pro-Am tourney was staging its games, The Future's colorful act began to go a bit black-and-white in a more structured offense, and the legion of fans, especially the ones who had followed him in worship from the playgrounds to the hardwood, were a little mystified and, quite frankly, disappointed.

"For the first time in my life I wasn't doing all the crazy, between-the-legs, behind-the-neck, behind-the-back stuff," The Future said. "I was trying to show my teammates and all the people who know me that I can play within a system, that I can handle myself indoors, against pros.

"I wanted them to know that I wasn't just some kind of carnival act," he said. "Indoors or outdoors, people need to know that I'm a sound ballplayer with a fundamental knowledge of the game."

Though some who had flocked to see him quickly turned into boo birds, The Future had made his point, helping Dyckman win a Pro-Am championship by defeating a Nike One squad run by Charles Jones.

By the end of the Pro-Am season, most fans were lining up after games for The Future's autograph. Some parents, certain The Future was on his way to the big show, even posed their children beside him for pictures.

But long after those pictures were developed, The Future still had not made the ultimate leap beyond the chain-link fences, where he had gained much fame and little fortune in Marvel-Comics-like clashes with streetball stars like Terminator, Sick One, Captain Nappy, and Predator.

While The Future has proven he is one of the few legitimate playground legends who could hold his own in the NBA, he is surely a victim of his own ego, held back by the same arrogance that is his staunch ally on the court, his bitter enemy off it.

A former star at James Monroe High School in the Bronx, The Future spent two years at Jacksonville Junior College in Texas and a year at Utah State before he dropped out.

"We started losing a lot, and guys were starting to get on my nerves," The Future explained to me during an interview I did for *Vibe* magazine on the history of Holcombe Rucker's paradise.

The Future still boasts a stellar amateur career that includes battles with NBA stars that rattle off his tongue like machine-gun fire: Stephon Marbury, Rafer Alston, Ray Allen, Nick Van Exel, Sam Cassell, Johnny Newman, Kenny Anderson, Baron Davis.

"The one I want now is Allen Iverson," The Future said. "I love his game. I love his heart."

The Future's résumé also includes a bunch of print, radio, and television ads he has done in recent years for Nike, which has put together a number of smart spots featuring playground legends from coast to coast.

Several years ago, after seeing The Future's dope game displayed on a TNT basketball documentary entitled "On Hallowed Ground," which looked at players and teams who perform at Rucker Park, Shaquille O'Neal himself went out of his way to call the playground legend, whom he had never met. The two soon became good friends, and Shaq placed a couple of calls to the International Basketball League, getting The Future a tryout with the Las Vegas Bandits.

"You have to start somewhere. You need a past to have a present," Shaq told The Future.

Despite Shaq's efforts, The Future blew off his tryout with

the Bandits, just the way Joe Hammond had blown off the Lakers thirty years before. He even sounded like Hammond when defending his choice not to take a shot with the Bandits.

"I didn't get any guarantees," said The Future, bursting with stubborn pride. "If I don't get a guarantee, why fly out west and waste any time when I can stay home and make up the money here?

"I'm the Michael Jordan of playground basketball," The Future explained. "I'm at the point in my career where teams should be coming to me and saying, 'Okay, Future, we know what you can do. Just show up and we'll put you down.'

"Look, all of them pros I played against give me love because they know I held my own against them," he said. "I dropped twenty-seven on Steph at Rucker, and everywhere I've gone after that, people on the streets kept telling me, 'Yo, Future, you gotta be playin' in the NBA.' It really frustrated me to hear that because I know I can play with these guys, and they know it, too."

And so The Future, stubborn and talented as ever, will be back at Rucker this summer, waiting for a Pat Riley or a Phil Jackson to take a seat in the hot, stone bleachers that overlook the tiny park and watch him do his thing.

"They might think I'm showboating out there, but that's because I'm playing in the Entertainers League, and all my moves are for the fans," he said. "But put me in an organized game, and you'll see that this kid is unstoppable. I've already proven that as well, just ask all them guys at the Pro-Am."

Now that he's thirty-something, it's awfully hard to tell a guy nicknamed The Future that his best ballin' days might be behind him. But it won't matter anyway because The Future, as always, is doing it his way, lacing up his hi-tops and taking bows on the big blacktop that Holcombe Rucker invented.

And just like every other asphalt god roaming that mythical stretch of basketball paradise across the street from the site of the old Polo Grounds, The Future is dreaming a near impossible dream, but one that he and legions of his fans can still taste on a hot day in Harlem.

Chapter 7

A "BUSINESS" IS BORN

y the summer of 1990, Greg Marius had perfected the formula that made his Entertainers Basketball Classic the top hoops tournament in the country. The combination of basketball and hip-hop music continued to bring out some of the top stars from each of those two worlds, slowly raising the league's profile to the kind of lofty heights that the Rucker Tournament had known in its heyday. Sponsorship money began to pour in from record labels like Puff Daddy's Bad Boy Entertainment, Cold Chillin', Def Jam, and Uptown Records, and before long, mainstream corporations like AT&T and Reebok were on board. Soon, NBA players and local products like Walter Berry and Mark Jackson of St. John's and Steve Burtt of Iona began coming back on a regular basis. The teams that now ran in the tournament played better, and looked better, as they were now outfitted with slick uniforms.

"That's when I noticed that what I had was really turning into a business," Marius said. "From there, my game plan was not to compete with anybody else's format, but to concentrate on what I do best. People kept telling me that if I wanted to be successful, I had to have a tournament like the one on West Fourth Street, where the games are very closely officiated. But I let the guys playing in my league do all the stuff they wanted to do out there with the basketball, like the fancy dribbling, for the sake of entertainment. And it worked."

That same year, Marius formed a partnership with a man named Robert "Gus" Wells, who was sponsoring a team in the EBC Tournament. Wells owned the Rooftop Disco, which was located just a block from Rucker Park.

"Gus was into hip-hop clubs, and since I started in music, things just began to click between us," Marius said. "I brought some acts I had known from my deejay days to Gus's club, and he taught me a lot about security, which I really needed in the park to make sure nothing ever got out of hand."

Marius now had enough money to give the hallowed asphalt a facelift. He repaved and repainted the Rucker court and put up sturdier baskets. With Wells as head of security, more than a dozen guards were hired to ring the court during each contest.

Marius and Wells then sat down with both the Department of Parks and the police department to work out the amount of security that would be provided by the city.

"It was hard to work that out at first, because the police just assumed I was a drug dealer," Marius said. "They thought that because we had reached a certain level of monetary success, we had to be selling drugs or doing something illegal. But once we laid it all out for them, told them how far along we had brought the tournament, they were ready to play ball."

When the talks ended, the police department agreed to dispatch twelve to fifteen officers per game to help maintain order in the park. The police also set up barricades before and after each game, and agreed to help direct traffic in and out of the park.

Despite all the costly changes, Marius refused to charge admission to the hundreds of people who crammed their bodies into the park each night to root on the action.

"Our fans don't pay. That's a park tradition," said Marius. "In fact, our fans are as much a part of the Rucker scene as our players. It's a community thing, a family-like gathering every night, and family doesn't pay."

The Best-Kept-Secret

To the people of Rucker Park, Kareem Reid will always be the Best-Kept-Secret.

By the age of fifteen, the tiny Bronx native had already earned his nickname twisting the ankles of grown men and whizzing no-look, behind-the-back passes to teammates twice his age and looking twice the size of this five-foot-six-inch, lightning-quick, left-handed blur.

By the summer of 1992, Reid, one of the greatest ball handlers ever to come out of the city, had transferred from defunct Tolentine High School to mighty St. Raymond's, another Catholic high school hoop power from the Bronx.

That same summer, Reid was joined in the backcourt on a squad named Mousey Dream Team by New York's other preeminent point guard, Stephon Marbury, a sensational fourteen-year-old Coney Islander starring for Lincoln High in Brooklyn, one of the city's top public school teams.

"They called us the wonder twins," said Reid, who has since grown to five feet eleven inches. "Playing in Rucker Park at such a young age was an incredible experience for both of us."

Playing for Mousey Dream Team in a regular season contest that year, Reid earned his Best-Kept nickname by launching a game-winning jumper over the outstretched fingertips of The Future himself, putting the finishing touches on a 50-point masterpiece that became Malloy Nesmith's most embarrassing moment.

"That kid came out of nowhere that day," recalled The Future. "After he hit that shot on me, you couldn't call him anything but Best-Kept-Secret."

Reid, who would lead St. Ray's to the city and state championship just one year later, looks back at that one game, and at that one thrilling facial of The Future, as a major turning point in what would become a brilliant basketball career.

"I went home that night and said to myself, 'Kareem, you did that against The Future,'" he said. "It was really amazing because he was The Future, I mean everybody knew about him. I showed The Future and all those fans my potential that day, and I proved a whole lot to myself as well. After that, I never, ever lost confidence in myself or doubted my own abilities on a basketball court."

Reid, who played at Arkansas from 1995 to 1999, nearly made Larry Bird's Indiana Pacers several seasons ago.

"But that was the year that Jalen Rose wanted to play the point," Reid said. "Wrong place, wrong time."

The Best-Kept-Secret rebounded with the Harlem Globetrotters, and he is one of the rare players who performs on the Trotters' show team as well as on their competitive team.

Now twenty-six, Reid lives in Arkansas as well as the Bronx. He has played professionally in Turkey, but is still hoping to get a handle on an NBA job. "I know I'm as good as or better than some of the guards in the NBA right now," he said. "I just need to be in the right situation, with the right people in my corner representing me. When I was a little younger, I didn't have that type of guidance."

Just two weeks before the NBA draft in June 1995, Reid's telephone started ringing. His doorbell began doing much the same, and voices from the street below began bouncing off his apartment windows in the Bronx.

"Everybody and their mother was looking for me that day," Reid said. "They wanted to tell me that Puffy brought Joe Smith to Rucker Park."

Indeed, Sean "Puff Daddy" Combs, CEO and president of Bad Boy Entertainment, was making good on a threat he'd made several weeks earlier. After a tough loss to Reid's Sugar Hill Gang, Puffy had a few choice words for the competition.

"I got somebody for ya'll," said Puff, smoke rising from his ego as he stormed off the court. "I got somebody, just wait."

That somebody was Joe Smith, the Emergency Man himself. The former Maryland star, projected by many hoopologists as the top pick in the land come the NBA's pick-a-millionaire festival, was joining forces with Maryland mate Exree Hipp and former St. John's guard Boo Harvey on Puffy's Bad Boys.

"When I walked into the park, nobody wanted to play the game because they said that Joe was a ringer and that he hadn't been on Puffy's roster from the start of the season," Reid said. "I said, 'So what, let's just play the game.'"

Teaming on the Sugar Hill squad with Al "Alimoe" Evans, a slippery-smooth six seven swingman from Cal Bakersfield, and Arthur Long, a six ten center who played at Cincinnati and would later latch on with the Seattle SuperSonics, the Best-Kept-Secret revealed his true greatness yet again, exploding for 38 points and 13 helpers on a night when a red-faced Puffy would finally realize that rapping was a whole lot better than yapping.

In the closing seconds of a tied game, the little man went deep once more, his long-range bull's-eye just clearing the fingernails of the Emergency Man and settling into the cords as time was running out. When the final horn sounded, Reid had cemented his place in Harlem folklore.

After the game, Puffy put his arm around Best-Kept-Secret in an attempt to join the man he could not beat. "You wanna get down with us next year?" Puffy asked Reid. "We'd love to have you on our side."

Two weeks later, NBA commissioner David Stern announced that Joe Smith of Maryland, the same Joe Smith that Kareem Reid took to hoops school in Rucker Park that summer, was being chosen by Golden State as the top overall selection in the draft.

Best-Kept-Secret was home, watching and hoop dreaming on his pillow.

"I was happy for Joe, and the fact that he went number one made that game I played against him even more special to me, and more special to the fans who were there that day," Reid said. "That was one of the biggest games I ever played, and not just because it was against Joe Smith.

"The truth is," Reid said, "that because of my height, people have always doubted my abilities on the court. But I think people stopped doubting me once and for all after that game. I think anyone who was watching learned that it doesn't matter the size of the man, but the size of the heart beating inside of him."

Best-Kept-Secret came oh-so-close to winning an EBC title in the summer of 1996, when he single-handedly led Sugar Hill to the finals after eliminating the X-Men with a 50-point explosion in a semifinal contest.

In the final seconds of that clash, Sugar Hill trailed the X-Men by two points when Reid took an inbounds pass beneath his own basket from Charles Jones. Immediately trapped by David Cain and Lamont Middleton, Reid dribbled out of trouble and sped up court. With one second left on the ticker, Reid pulled up from another area code and, over the leaping paws of The Animal, Richie Adams, somehow managed to elevate high enough to launch a long three-pointer that found the bottom of the net and gave Sugar Hill a wild one-point victory and a ticket to the championship game.

"The fans came storming out on the court to hug me," Reid said. "I just laid there, exhausted, while everyone around me was just going crazy."

But the title game between Sugar Hill and Flavor Unit never came off, as an estimated five thousand spectators got league officials and the New York City Police Department more than a little worried. The game was canceled due to the overcrowded conditions, which had led to some fighting hours before the contest even began.

To the best of most memories, this was the first game canceled in Rucker Park since overcrowding forced the Pied Piper himself to call off that 1960 affair to be played by Connie Hawkins and his Brooklyn buddy, Roger Brown.

"That was my best shot at winning it all," Reid said at the time. "But I'll be back, because I have a lot of basketball left inside of me."

Five years later the little man with the big heart was tearing up Rucker Park. Playing for Puffy's Bad Boys in the summer of 2001, Reid became the first player in the history of Rucker Park to lead the league in points (29.7) and assists (8) per game for an entire season. Ironically enough, he dropped 38 points dur-

ing his record-setting season against Jamaal "Mel Mel The
Abuser" Tinsley, the former Iowa guard and Rucker great who
now runs the point for, you guessed it, the Indiana Pacers.

Best-Kept-Secret said he has also dropped 40 on Stephon
Marbury "a couple of times," and during his record run gave the
same treatment in one game to Joe Smith of the Minnesota Timberwolves and Kenny Satterfield of the Denver Nuggets, who
teamed in the backcourt with the Ruff Ryders.

Reid said he hopes to one day parlay his Rucker and Globetrotter success into an NBA job. "Hey," said Best-Kept-Secret, "I
got goals, and I'm still young enough to achieve them."

Big Stretch

Larry Elting was also young enough to achieve the goals he had
set for himself when he crossed prison paths with Joe Hammond
on Rikers Island in the summer of 1993.

"You better come out here and watch this kid play," Hammond told me that summer. "This kid's got some kind of game.
He writes me letters all the time, asking me if I know anybody
who might be able to get him back into basketball. I told him all
about you."

Just three weeks earlier, I had already visited Hammond at
Rikers. By the time the Department of Corrections was able to
get me a new visit with Elting, he had already been released,
committed another crime, and had been sent north to Cox-
sackie. That's where I found him eight months later.

By now Elting was the star center for Crazy II, the basketball
squad that represented the fifty-four men who lived in the C2
dormitory. Crazy II had just lost the championship of Greene Fa-

cility's Recreational League. Elting and company were one of twenty teams that fought for three months to capture the league's top prize: a pizza party.

I wrote about Elting in *Slam* magazine and later in the *New York Times*. I wrote about an undisciplined six-foot-nine-inch kid with basketball talent who got into a gunfight in his hometown of Poughkeepsie, New York, in March 1991 and had been in and out of prison since that time for committing a number of other crimes. And I wrote about a remorseful and sincere young man who was taking college-level courses in prison, and how he desperately wanted another chance to get his life back on track and to play organized basketball again. The four-page article in *Slam*, entitled "Redemption Song: Sometimes You Need to Fall to Learn How to Fly," caught the attention of a number of college coaches across America, and many of them flocked to that prison schoolyard to scout his games. By the time Elting was set free in May 1995, he had a number of scholarship offers to consider. He chose to play in 1996 at Westchester Community College, where he had to "learn the fundamentals of the game all over again."

The following year he transferred to Dean College in Franklin, Massachusetts, where he played his last year of collegiate ball. Elting, now married, dropped out of college in 1998 to jump at a job offer from IBM, where he planned "on being an executive there" by the time he was thirty-five years old.

But Larry Elting still had a lot of basketball left inside him and continued to play basketball whenever and wherever he could.

By the summer of 2001, Elting, then twenty-eight and a service delivery manager at IBM, was recruited by yet another team, this one called Cash Money Millionaires. Cash Money, one of the elite teams playing in Rucker Park that summer, boasted such stars as former St. John's and current Indiana Pacer Ron Artest, and Charles Jones, who twice led the nation in scoring at LIU and had logged a few NBA minutes of his own.

Cash Money had been searching for a big man to get them over the championship hump, and Larry Elting was their man.

"I couldn't believe that after all these years, I was finally playing in Rucker Park," Elting said. "At first, I was in such awe of the crowd, such awe of my teammates and all the other great players I was competing against, guys like Mark Jackson and Steve Francis. In my own little way, it was like, 'Wow, I've finally arrived.' "

Cash Money and "Big Stretch," the Rucker nickname bestowed upon Elting, lost just one of twelve games that summer and rolled along to win their first Entertainers Championship.

"We had been to the championship game at Rucker the summer before, but lost," said O. J. Sumter, aka "The Show Stopper," a six seven forward who teamed with Elting on Cash Money and went on to star at Palm Beach Community College in Lake Worth, Florida. "But we put it all together in 2001."

One of the courtside guests at Rucker Park that summer was Shaquille O'Neal, who applauded the fine work of fellow big men Big Stretch and The Show Stopper after one regular season contest during Cash Money's march to glory.

"Seeing Shaq there was a major lift for all of us," The Show Stopper said. "If you earned his respect out there on the court, you know you did something right."

A number of those games, now played with the NBA's blessings and seen on satellite television, were beamed back to Larry Elting's hometown. In Poughkeepsie, where some people once compared his clan to the notorious Clantons, the words "Elting" and "court" now had a completely different association.

"The best part of that whole experience was going back home after the season ended," Big Stretch said. "People were stopping me on the streets and saying they had seen me playing at Rucker Park on TV. These were the same people who used to give me funny looks when I walked past them years earlier, when I was in all that trouble.

"One older woman made my journey complete," Big Stretch said, "by saying that she was really proud of me."

Saying Good-bye

In May of 1998, a sobbing Joe Hammond called to tell me that Earl Manigault had seen his last sunset. The Goat, fifty-three, died of congestive heart failure in Manhattan's Bellevue Hospital. The Destroyer, by the Goat's side to witness his final breath, cried like a baby when his schoolyard chum passed. I was assigned the difficult task of writing the Goat's obituary in the *New York Times*. Having met him and admired his courage and candor, I felt I owed him, at the very least, parting words that justified his existence, that made him more important than just a player who jumped higher than most everyone else around him. My editors let the obituary run 764 words, a flattering length for a player who never made the leap from the schoolyard to the pros.

"In storied matchups against other stars like Alcindor, Connie Hawkins and Joe 'The Destroyer' Hammond," I wrote, "Manigault helped enhance New York's playground legend as a breeding ground for young stars.

"Although he was relatively small at six feet one inch, he had a remarkable leaping ability that allowed him to soar over taller opponents, as well as an array of flashy moves under the basket," the obit continued. "It was this kind of exhibition that sent fans flocking to any park where Manigault was playing, especially to places like Rucker Park in Harlem and the playground at 99th Street and Amsterdam Ave. that came to be known as Goat Park. It was there that Manigault honed his reputation as a showman and hustler. He would win bets against those who refused to believe that the mighty springs in his legs could enable him to pick a quarter off the top of a backboard."

Perhaps no one put Manigault's death in better perspective than Joe Hammond did.

"Earl's death marks the end of an era on the playgrounds of New York City," Hammond told me. "How many playground legends, I mean guys who made their reps in the parks and nowhere else, drew the kinds of crowds that Earl did? I mean, no one was reading about this guy in the sports section every day, but people all around the city had found out about him by word of mouth, and when they went to go see what everyone else was talking about, they weren't disappointed.

"The Goat was one of the great showmen of his time," Hammond said. "And it's a damn shame that most people never got a chance to watch this guy soar on a basketball court. They ought to hang one of his old jerseys way up on a lamp post at Rucker Park for all the world to see."

Indeed, few playground legends had earned the amount of fan and media attention that the Goat had. In 1989, long after drugs had stripped him of his great athletic ability and forced a premature end to his playing days, a *New York Times* reporter, Ian O'Connor, observed that the Goat was still being treated like royalty on the same streets where his great potential had disappeared.

"Manigault hardly looks like a hero," O'Connor wrote. "At 6 feet 1 inch and 175 pounds, he is not a particularly big man. He moves through the park with a cigarette hanging from his mouth, carrying a can of beer in a brown paper bag and sipping through a straw. He is dressed in a faded T-shirt and blue shorts. He hunches slightly when he walks. But while the neighborhood residents now see a shell of the athlete they once idolized, they also remember the pride he brought to them.

"As the 44-year-old Manigault walks through the small park, only a few blocks from where he grew up, he is instantly recognized. Everyone he passes approaches Manigault to offer greetings. . . . Manigault's personality is one of the reasons the neighborhood people still treat him with reverence. Despite all his failures, he is still regarded as a king of sorts, a ruler of the two blocks that connect Goat Park to Frederick Douglass Playground on 100th Street."

A week after my obit ran, Peter Vecsey, whose early years in journalism were also spent coaching basketball legends like Julius Erving up at Rucker Park, paid tribute to the Goat in his "Hoop Du Jour" column in the *New York Post*: "The pertinence of Frank Sinatra and Earl Manigault dying a week-and-a-half ago, within hours of each other, is inescapable," Vecsey wrote. "One man sang 'Fly Me to the Moon.' The other man jumped to the moon."

Skip-To-My-Lou

In the early 1990s, one of the best ever to play at Rucker Park, maybe even the best, was a skinny, dark-skinned kid from South Jamaica, Queens, named Rafer Alston, better known to his Rucker audience as Skip-To-My-Lou.

In a sense, Skip-To-My-Lou, whose nickname describes his ability to dribble-dance by helpless defenders, was the last Joe Hammond figure, the last true playground legend to take that magic carpet ride from the Pied Piper's paradise to a chance at the big show.

"People always tell me that I'm the last of the great line of street legends to make it to the NBA," Alston said. "Hey, if I'm following in the footsteps of guys like Joe Hammond and Pee Wee Kirkland, well, that's company I can be proud of."

Late in the summer of 1995, Skip-To-My-Lou, who split his high school ball between Cardozo in Queens and Laurinburg Institute in North Carolina, was doing his thing at Holcombe Rucker's place, collecting oohhs and ahhs with every crossover dribble, every spin move in the lane, every look-away pass. Shoelaces were popping all over the yard.

One of those happy onlookers was Jerry Tarkanian, the Shark himself, who had circled back on New York's streetball scene two decades after sinking his teeth into Sidney Green and Richie Adams, hauling both of them out west.

By now the Shark was no longer at UNLV, but at Fresno State, and in Skip-To-My-Lou he again smelled the kind of city game that once helped transform the Runnin' Rebels into a national hoop power.

"Somebody told me that night that Coach Tarkanian was in

the stands," Alston said. "I didn't look at it as an audition or anything. I just went out there and played my game."

The Shark liked what he saw.

One week later he contacted the young court magician and talked him into heading west.

"He loved everything about my game," Alston said of Tarkanian. "He loved my handle, he loved my speed, and he loved the way I got up and put pressure on the ball."

The following year, Alston was enrolled at Fresno Junior City College, and by the 1997–98 college campaign, he was running the point for Shark's Fresno State squad.

The magic carpet ride continued, and two seasons later Rafer Alston was a second-round draft choice of the Milwaukee Bucks.

Though Hammond and Kirkland were drafted by NBA teams, their respective dreams eventually died. But Skip-To-My-Lou went to Bucks camp and showed that coaching staff what he had shown the people at Rucker Park for years, the kind of wicked stuff that had the Shark circling back east for big-city skills. He made the team and then some, playing with the Bucks for the next three seasons. He split the 2002–3 NBA season with Golden State and Toronto.

"The road was long," Alston said. "Fortunately for me, I had a unique stage to show the world what I was capable of doing. And for that, I have Holcombe Rucker to thank."

The Wolverine

One June evening in 1996, the Mousey Dream Team was short-staffed. Rather than forfeit to the late Conrad "McNasty"

McRae's Sports Entourage squad, Mousey Carella enlisted the
help of a shy but chiseled hoop warrior beaming in the twilight.

No one knew him, though he looked familiar. Mousey, who is
to head coaching at Rucker what head coaches like Lenny
Wilkens, Pat Riley, and Phil Jackson are to the NBA, thinks he
may have seen the diesel-sized, six seven, 220-pounder with the
light chocolate skin and movie-star good looks on television
somewhere, or maybe he'd seen him at another park, in another
league. The nameless player couldn't be a day older than twenty-
two, though he had the physical makeup of a seasoned pro and
carried himself in the far reaches of the park with the kind of
quiet confidence that had Mousey scurrying his way just a few
minutes before the opening tip.

"Yo, what's your name?" Mousey asked the unknown soldier.

The young man paused for a second, looked to the heavens as
if he were searching the windy skies for the right answer, then
replied softly: "They call me Wolverine."

"We're one man short tonight," Mousey said to Wolverine.
"You look like a player. Wanna get down with us?"

The Wolverine never said another word. He simply smiled
and pulled over his wide frame a royal blue jersey that was a part
of the uniform Mousey and company wore in basketball combat.

"McNasty and them boys had never seen this kid before," said
Duke "Tango" Mills, the man behind the microphone that
evening. "I heard them asking one another if anyone knew anything about him, and everyone was just kind of shaking their
head like, 'Nah, man, ain't never seen him.' "

His own teammates had not seen Wolverine play a minute of
basketball, either, yet he was chosen to jump against McNasty
to start the contest.

The Wolverine won the opening tip, and on Mousey's first possession took a pass along the right baseline, rose over McNasty's fingernails, and into a swirling wind, let loose a rainbow jumper that did not wrinkle the net when falling through it.

"Yo, who dat?" someone yelled from behind the Entourage bench.

Cheers of appreciation rising from the crowd, both teams went the other way, and McNasty demanded the rock. He took a pass at the foul line, stormed past Wolverine and two other players with a fury, and assaulted the rim with a vicious one-handed dunk that put a soft smile on Wolverine's face.

At halftime of a close game, no one knew where Wolverine had gone. A panicked Mousey looked around the small park but couldn't find his late addition. Then, just before the start of the second half, Wolverine reappeared. No one knew where he had gone.

But the unknown soldier had reenlisted for another half of basketball duty, and long into the night, his legendary battle with McNasty continued. The Wolverine did most of his damage from the ground, launching long-range bombs from everywhere on the court while McNasty attacked most often from the air, putting several dents in the bright orange steel rims.

In the closing seconds of a tied game, Wolverine took a pass deep in the right corner and faded back for what appeared to be another long-range missile strike. An Entourage player who had gotten lost on a switch in the heat of the battle ran out toward Wolverine, leaping high to block his shot. But the Wolverine pulled the ball down, and as the defender flew past him, took two hard dribbles toward the rim and went airborne on his final attack.

McNasty left his defensive position at the top of the key and sped toward the basket to cut down the Wolverine, who was now in midair, ball held high with both hands over his head.

Somewhere above the rim, high over the battlefield, both players met. McNasty attempted to block the shot but the Wolverine had a bit more hangtime to his flight, and as McNasty began his descent, the Wolverine fell out of the sky and slammed tomahawk-style as the final buzzer sounded.

The crowd erupted and spilled onto the court in celebration. Mousey, McNasty, and players from both teams began looking through the crowd to congratulate Wolverine for a superhero-like performance, but somehow he had already disappeared into the night.

No one ever saw him again.

Puffy's Dynamic Duo

The very same month that Wolverine made his mark, another hard to imagine sight surfaced at the Rucker.

Imagine if you will, Larry Bird and Magic Johnson teaming in the same backcourt, on a playground no less, just days before those superstars were selected in the NBA draft. A joined force of such magnitude took place at Rucker Park in June of 1996, when Allen Iverson, the great point guard from Georgetown who would become the top overall draft pick that season, teamed with Stephon Marbury, the Brooklyn basketball prodigy who had starred at Lincoln High School before moving on to Georgia Tech and becoming a first-round pick in the same draft.

"As if they were in a jazz band," wrote David Cummings of the

New York Daily News, "Marbury and Iverson took turns going on personal solo acts—but this was much more of a hip-hop performance."

With stars such as Queen Latifah and then L.A. Clipper Malik "The Freak" Sealy watching from courtside, and a lucky-to-be-there, overflow crowd spilling onto the painted white lines that surround the fabled court, Iverson and Marbury put on a show that painted a huge smile on the face of Sean "Puff Daddy" Combs, who had arranged to bring both stars together to play for his Bad Boys squad against Sugar Hill, a team led by the Best-Kept-Secret, Kareem Reid.

Able to spread their talented wings without playing in a caged system run by a college or professional coach, the six one Iverson, aka The Answer, and the six two Marbury, aka The Handler, took turns practicing their own brand of magic in the warm Harlem air.

Iverson, who had already dished out eye-opening assists and taken his man off the dribble for several breathtaking drives to the rim early in the game, carved his legend into the historic blacktop late in the first half.

The Answer took a pass from The Handler at half-court, zipped toward the basket, and elevated just outside the dotted lines. While rising, Iverson held the ball in his right hand, brought it down to his stomach, and then, the mighty springs in his legs still keeping him afloat, raised the ball a second time and slammed it through the basket.

Ecstatic fans had inched so close to the court that Iverson literally fell into the crowd after his fantabulous flush. A number of fans hugged The Answer before sending him back into the game.

"Before that game, I thought Iverson was just another gunner," Cummings said, "but I realized that day that this guy had the whole package, that he could do anything he wanted on a basketball court that was needed of him."

A few possessions later, it was The Handler's turn.

Marbury took a pass from The Answer near the sideline at half-court. With defenders between him and the basket, The Handler made his way through heavy traffic and dribbled three times, loud and hard enough to momentarily drown out the crowd noise, before hitting the runway with the rock firmly gripped in his right hand. The Handler floated past one defender, fluttered high above the tin as if he were going to answer The Answer with a flush of his own, but decided instead to simply flick his wrist for an easy finger roll.

"I never saw Dr. J. and those guys play," Cummings said. "But of all the games I've ever seen at Rucker Park, that one, with all the great dunking and passing and dribbling, with all of those alley-oop passes, was easily the greatest."

When showtime was over, The Answer had 40 points and The Handler added 20. But only on the kind of talented stage that Holcombe Rucker created could a combined 60-point performance by two future NBA superstars not be enough.

Incredibly, the Bad Boys lost that evening on what turned out to be a game-winning jumper by the Best-Kept-Secret. The game was called late in the fourth quarter when a fight broke out in the stands. No one was seriously hurt, but The Answer didn't stick around long enough to ask any questions. The dynamic guard slipped out of the park unscathed, hopped into a golden Mercedes with Virginia license plates that was waiting for him behind the chain-link fence, and sped south toward the Benjamin Franklin Bridge with a few of his boys.

After Best-Kept-Secret hit what turned out to be the game-winning jumper that sent The Answer, The Handler, and Puff Daddy home with lots of memories but no bragging rights, Coach Puff was in a huff.

"We were going full tilt, no excuses," Puff Daddy told me a few years later. "We learned that night that you can get your ass waxed in Rucker if you don't come into the park in the right frame of mind and ready to play."

If the filmmaker Spike Lee is the patron celebrity saint of the New York Knicks, then Sean "Puffy" Combs is the patron celebrity saint of those other Bad Boys from New York City, the team uptown that the man now known as P. Diddy has been sponsoring and coaching for nearly a decade in Rucker Park.

"I would say I go to about 50 percent of the games each season," says P. Diddy, who does hoop battle against other Rucker squads coached and owned by the likes of fellow-rappers Fat Joe and Ja Rule.

"Most of the community up there knows me because they knew me when I was coming up in that area," he said. "I grew up on 145th Street and Lenox Avenue, so to them I'm just another local guy, and it ain't no big deal to have me in the park."

P. Diddy has been going to games at Rucker Park since he grew up in Harlem, and when his family moved to Mount Vernon, he rode the train back to his old stomping grounds to keep up with the action.

"I was following the Rucker long before I became a star," he says. "I just think that it's such an incredibly positive thing for the neighborhood. Up there, people are yearning for positive recreation. Not all of them have such easy lives, and this makes their lives a little happier. It's something they can be proud of because it doesn't exist in any other neighborhood."

Over the years, P. Diddy has used his star status to attract some of the best players ever to the land of the Pied Piper. The Bad Boys have featured playground stars like "The Future" Malloy Nesmith, the "Best-Kept-Secret" Kareem Reid (jumping ship), Shamgod Wells, "The Terminator" Ronnie Mathias, and Marshall "Up North" Grier, a six five scoring forward out of Ryder University.

Puff Daddy (aka P. Diddy), bottom right, with his Bad Boys team
(Rodney Williams)

The team's professional stable has included the likes of Joe Smith and, of course, Marbury and Iverson.

"The guys who have impressed me the most though, in addition to Kareem Reid," says P. Diddy, "have been playground stars like Wali 'The Main Event' Dixon, and that kid Adrian Walton

that they call 'Whole Lotta Game'—I seen him take Stephon
Marbury to school out there."

For P. Diddy there are two motivating forces that keep him
coming back to the historic park.

"One is to provide entertainment to the community in an atmosphere that can only be provided by this community," he says.
"If you played this tournament in the UCLA gym on the West
Coast, it wouldn't have the same effect as playing it outdoors
across from the Polo Grounds, because there is so much history
attached to it, so much love and respect for the game and for the
players.

"The second motivation, and I'll be straight here," says P.
Diddy, "is to win. It's all about pride. My teams go in there to win
because the Rucker is the most competitive, most prestigious,
and most historic summer league out there. I mean, you have
guys like Joe Hammond, who had big games thirty years ago, and
people are still talking about him till this day. He's a living legend because he made his rep at the Rucker against great players
like Dr. J."

Spike can keep his expensive courtside seat at the World's
Most Famous Arena, because P. Diddy is more comfortable,
more at home, strolling the sidelines of the world's most famous
playground.

"I'd rather watch a Rucker game than an NBA game," says P.
Diddy. "It's much more exciting. You could be in the NBA and
still get your ass busted in Rucker Park."

P. Diddy has twice climbed to the top of the asphalt heap, winning two EBC Championships during his long association with
Rucker Park. Those two titles mean as much to him, he said, as
anything he has ever accomplished in the world of music.

"To win a Rucker championship means that you're the best, period," says P. Diddy. "It means you're the kings of the playground, and it's a great feeling.

"That said, though," P. Diddy adds, "I must tell you that the things that define the Rucker's overall greatness are not the teams who've won championships, but the great individual matchups throughout history like Hammond against Dr. J., or Pee Wee Kirkland against Tiny Archibald, or Skip-To-My-Lou against The Future.

"It's those individual matchups, or certain team matchups during one particular night, stuff like that, that make the league so special and so unique."

P. Diddy reminded me that as glamorous as performing on Holcombe Rucker's stage has been for most players over the years, it has been that much more frustrating and humiliating for those players who simply melted beneath the heat of the bright lights, those players who do not own a page in history's scrapbook.

"These guys have to somehow keep their heads on straight while they're dealing with all of that heckling," he says. "It's like playing the Apollo Theater on a Wednesday night, with all of those hecklers—it's not easy to keep your composure."

P. Diddy, who puts his summer rosters together "with the help of some cats I roll with or the recommendations of some of my coaches," also noted that competing for the best record on the asphalt is quite different from competing for the best record on the hip-hop charts.

"It's a completely different kind of competition," he says. "It's a whole different type of status to be considered the best on the playgrounds as opposed to being the best rapper or something like that. Music and basketball are both cool, they complement each other, but you really can't mix them like that."

In the end, says P. Diddy, every player who has ever laced up his sneaks in Rucker Park, no matter his pro or playground status, no matter his height or weight or color or politics or geographic origin—all of them have one thing in common.

"They have heart," P. Diddy said. "That is the true definition of a streetball player—heart. That is the true definition of a New York player—heart."

Pay for Play

Most of the players who compete today at Rucker Park, especially the great ones, play for pay. This is a subject not often written or talked about openly. There are, however, exceptions.

In the colorful history of hoops at the Pied Piper's place, where some basketball tales seem to grow taller by the dribble, there is no exaggeration attached to the kind of salary commanded, if not demanded, by James "Speedy" Williams in the past decade.

"I'm good for six or seven hundred dollars a game, not including bonuses," says Speedy. "If you ain't gonna give me what I'm worth out there, then don't even bother calling me."

Still lightning-quick after blowing out all thirty-six candles on his birthday cake, Speedy had been given that nickname when it was realized that he could cover ninety-four feet of hardwood faster than most anyone else playing the game.

Speedy was a star at Medgar Evers College in Brooklyn, where he averaged a team-high 26 points per contest in the 1990–91 season, leading the City University of New York Conference in several major scoring categories.

Throughout the years at Rucker Park, Speedy has bolted from team to team with the highest payrolls. The man who played himself in the 1994 hoop drama *Above the Rim* is one of the few players to go on record and admit that he is part of the play-for-pay tradition that has been shrouded in secrecy since the inception of the EBC.

"Things are different now," Pete Vecsey says. "In the old days, guys just played for pride. The best players showed up from all over the city, or the country, just for the sake of competing against the best. Bob Love of the Chicago Bulls used to fly in on the weekends for games and stay at my place. He never asked for a dime."

Vecsey did remember one player back in the early 1970s who thought his appearance might yield some of the long green.

"Julius Erving's very first game at Rucker Park," Vecsey recalled. "He came over to me before the game and asked, 'Peter, how much am I getting paid today?' I just looked at him and said, 'Julius, it just doesn't work that way around here.' "

It does now.

When the world of entertainment came along to save Holcombe Rucker's baby, a new breed of player began to sprout through the cracks of his asphalt stage. If players like Speedy Williams were there to entertain, then they were going to get paid for their valuable time.

The big paydays, according to Speedy, are made possible by coaches and team owners. Even benchwarmers earn two to three hundred dollars per game, he said.

"You basically have three types of people in charge of the games out there," Speedy said. "You have the drug dealers who pay the players well, and you have the rappers who also pay well.

"Even the guys who make an honest living," Speedy said, "know they have to pay their guys."

Speedy, who has earned a living in basketball playing semi-professionally for ten seasons in the United States Basketball League and touring with the Harlem Wizards—the second-oldest show-team behind the Harlem Globetrotters—said that most coaches or team owners who pay their players hope to get huge returns on those investments from monster side bets that are made in the park on an almost nightly basis.

On an overcast day in the summer of 1997, one of those huge bets was placed on Speedy, who was turning heads and raising eyebrows with Absolute Power, a team that also included the "Natural Born Controller" Kerry Thompson, John "The Franchise" Strickland, and Shamel Jones, a lean, six-foot-seven-inch tower of power who had played at Memphis.

"We had one of the biggest payrolls out there that summer," Speedy said. "I remember the park being jam-packed, and guys from our team throwing Absolute Power T-shirts up into the stands to get the crowd rooting for us."

With the clouds going dark but holding tight, Absolute Power was locked in a seesaw battle with Die Hard, led by the legendary "Terminator," Ronnie Mathias, a six three swingman with a scorer's mentality who plowed through opponents and often left carnage on his many rumbles to the rack, and an offensive-minded madman known only as "Nutta Butter."

"This kid used to go nuts shooting out there, but he had a smooth, sweet shot, and whenever he made one, we'd always say, 'Man, that shot was butter,' " Speedy explained. "So we just started calling him Nutta Butter."

According to Speedy, roughly $10,000 in wagers had been

placed on the big game that day. With so much hanging in the balance, Absolute Power found itself trailing Die Hard by a single point with just seconds left on the game clock. (John "The Franchise" Strickland, a former star at Hawaii Pacific who always had trouble making free throws, was given an extra $100 for every basket made from the charity stripe during that game.)

As the final seconds ticked away, Absolute Power inbounded the ball at half-court.

The Natural Born Controller stormed ahead in an attempt to attack Die Hard's zone defense. Unable to penetrate to the rim, Kerry Thompson pulled up at the left side of the elbow, beneath the free throw line, and found Speedy in the right corner with a crisp pass that made its way through a maze of flailing arms.

Speedy caught the rock, and as The Terminator ran out to contest his long shot, Speedy let fly with just one tick left on the electric scoreboard.

A high-arcing rainbow shot that seemed to touch the dark clouds before traveling south, Speedy's offering finally fluttered back down to earth. As soon as the ball landed safely and softly through the cords, the skies opened up and Rucker Park became one huge shower stall.

"It was like Speedy's shot took the plug out of those clouds," said Duke "Tango" Mills, behind the mike for that classic moment as well. "Or maybe the basketball gods were just crying because they thought that shot was so sweet." The rain was still falling when someone slipped Speedy his bonus.

"One thousand dollars," Speedy said. "Not bad for one day's work, huh?"

General Electric Lights It Up

Every professional player who has ever passed through Rucker Park has locked horns with playground rivals like Speedy and Terminator, a woulda-coulda-shoulda alternate-universe image of himself who still haunts his pro counterpart in the scariest of asphalt dreams.

Wilt Chamberlain had his Cal Ramsey. Julius Erving had his Joe Hammond, and Tiny Archibald had his Pee Wee Kirkland. In more recent years, Stephon Marbury got a good look at The Future, Malloy Nesmith, and Rafer Alston had trouble catching a little lightning bolt named Earvin Opong, otherwise known as "I'll Be Right Back."

In the late summer of 1999, Jerry Stackhouse, the stellar six six swingman of the Washington Wizards who was playing then with the Detroit Pistons, got toasted by General Electric on back-to-back nights.

The regular season finale between Ed Lover's All-Stars—named after the popular radio host—and Flavor Unit was three minutes old when Stackhouse entered the park during a noisy time-out. The former North Carolina star, there to team on the Flavor Unit squad with blacktop legends like Kerry Thompson, Tony Greer, John "The Franchise" Strickland, Seth Marshall, and Shawnelle Scott, glared over at Ed Lover's bench on the way to his own.

"What really pissed me off," said Junie "General Electric" Sanders, "was that he showed up late, walked over to the wrong bench, and then gave us a nasty look like, 'I'm about to give you guys problems.' I didn't like it at all."

From that moment on, General Electric and company were

supercharged. Sanders, a Brooklyn kid who earned his nickname by lighting up opponents everywhere he played, had first made his bones at Central Oklahoma from 1993 to 1995. On this night the six four shooting guard, a veteran of the USBL, had already gotten into an offensive rhythm, scoring 5 points in the first three minutes.

"As soon as Stackhouse got into the game," General Electric said, "I greeted him with a three."

General Electric was getting started. He began lighting up the scoreboard with three-pointers from different area codes, and at one point midway through the first half lost Stackhouse with a blink-of-an-eye crossover in the left corner. With Stackhouse down for the count, General Electric turned the power up and stormed toward the hoop, rising high to lay the ball over the long arms of Scott and into the bucket. The crowd went wild.

"I wasn't starstruck by his presence," Sanders said of Stackhouse. "I get up for games like that because it gives me an opportunity to measure my game against the very best."

Throughout the game, General Electric continued to pile on the points. Players and coaches from Flavor Unit began getting on the officials for not giving their star player enough calls on his many trips to the tin.

When the final buzzer sounded, General Electric finished with a game-high 39 points, leading the charge to a wire-to-wire victory. "Any given day, if you come out and you're not prepared to play in the street, you'll be in trouble, because somebody will give you numbers," General Electric said. "When I saw the tape of that game, it was kind of funny to see that stunned look on Stack's face."

Less than twenty-four hours after their memorable encounter, Stackhouse and General Electric crossed wires again, this time indoors, at a Pro-Am game in New York.

"He saw me and didn't seem to mind," Sanders said of Stackhouse. "But I thought to myself, 'Oh no, here we go again.' "

Incredibly, General Electric was able to turn up the wattage for round two. Already averaging 40-plus points that season on a team called Nike One, General Electric exploded for 45 more, bringing his two-day point tally against Stackhouse, an NBA All-Star, to 84.

"Look, I know I'm not even in that guy's league," Sanders said. "But for those two games, I felt like I had made my mark in basketball in the inner city. I think that when people look back, they'll say it was a pretty big part of the playground legacy I left behind."

Air Canada

The Rucker legacy that Vince Carter left behind lasted all of one magical day. We waited and waited that day, thousands of us looking north all the while, hoping that maybe he'd fall out of the darkening skies above Rucker Park. We waited for any sign of Carter, aka Air Canada, who was scheduled to touch down on the hallowed blacktop early that August evening in 1999.

The rumor on the streets of our city was that the Raptors superstar, coming off his rookie of the year season, was flying south of the border that day, but the only things falling from the clouds now were huge, thick raindrops bouncing off the stone bleachers with the kind of force that suggested Mother Nature was in one of her moods again.

When lightning and a swirling wind entered the park, it was time for all of us to leave, time to head indoors, to the nearby Gauchos Gym in the Bronx where the nightcap would be played. The foul weather most certainly had fouled up his plans. Air Canada had been blown off course.

Once indoors, the playoff game between Blackhand Entertainment and Vacant Lot got under way. We were all under one roof now, watching one dynamite game, but there was still a bit of disappointment in the air. Air Canada not being there had taken some of the wind out of our collective sails. Even the rapper Jay-Z, strolling the sidelines like an expectant father, looked a bit bummed.

Late in the first quarter of that game, our eyes were fixed on the action when the man behind the microphone suddenly shrieked, bringing a once-famous Rucker Park call out of retirement: "HEEEEEE'S HEEEEEERE!"

Like a Marvel superhero, the Raptors superstar burst through the locker room doors to a deafening roar. Dressed in the brown-and-white battle fatigues of Blackhand Entertainment, Air Canada pleaded with the guy at the scorer's table to sound the substitution horn. After all, he had flown from the Great White North to be with this great, mostly black crowd, and was ready to soar smack into New York City's hoop history.

En route to 28 points of pure theater, Air Canada spread his wings over the competition with a third-quarter performance our grandchildren's grandchildren will be talking about. He scored 8 points in one minute, then ten more over the next nine minutes for an unforgettable 18-point explosion in ten minutes. Stay with me on the math, junior, because here is the stuff that history is made of:

- With 8 minutes 41 seconds to play in the third, Air Canada scoops up a loose ball in the paint and assaults the rim with a thunderous, two-handed jam for his first basket of the evening.

- With 8:05 left in the third, Air Canada, guarded by Charles Jones, takes a pass on the wing. He rises to take a jump shot on the left side of the floor, about twenty-three feet from the basket, and buries a three-pointer.

- With 7:41 to play in the third, Air Canada appears to be under lock and key, guarded tightly by a high school phenom from the Bronx named Adrian Walton, aka "Whole Lotta Game." Dribbling to a stop at the same spot where he'd nailed a three-pointer only seconds earlier, Air Canada gives Whole Lotta Game a cute little head fake followed by a ball fake, which causes the youngster to leave his feet. Alone for an instant, Air Canada lets fly again, burning the bottom of the cords from the exact same spot, which gives him 8 points in one minute—and he's just warming up.

- With 6:28 left in the third, Air Canada, teaming with a Washington, D.C., legend known as "The Prime Objective," aka Lonnie Harrell, breaks into the open court. Air Canada slips past one defender with a right-to-left, behind-the-back dribble, whips a behind-the-back pass left-to-right to a trailing Prime Objective, points toward Toronto, and as an alley-oop pass comes falling out of the sky, turns his body 180 degrees in midair so that he is facing the opposite basket, catches the rock, and throws it down with a force that literally shakes the Rucker faithful out onto the floor in celebration.

- With 3:41 left in the quarter and the building about to come apart at the seams, Air Canada loses Charles Jones off a high

Vince Carter lighting it up, throwing it down (*Michael Schmelling*)

screen by Prime Objective and slips out to the top of the key, behind the three-point stripe. *Swish*.

- With 1:28 left in the quarter, Air Canada feels too many bodies in the low post and curls out of the paint. He drifts deep in the left corner, catches a pass, and rises for a jumper. Can he connect on his sixth straight field goal attempt? Count it.

- There are 54 seconds left in the quarter, and like all great showmen, Air Canada has saved his best for the grand finale. The Rucker fans are still trying to catch their breath when Air Canada takes off again. As the final seconds begin to tick away, he rises to catch another alley-oop pass with his right hand along the left baseline, about five feet from the rim, and, still airborne, his back to the basket, slams windmill-style over the outstretched paws of two opponents, perhaps the greatest dunk in the history of the fabled tournament.

• When the final buzzer sounds, the crowd pours onto the court again, and this time the festivities last nearly ten minutes.

With thousands of stunned spectators chasing his taillights out into a rainy summer night, Air Canada gets back on the runway, heading north.

Chapter 8

A NEW CENTURY DAWNS

Picking up the scent of eight-foot-high championship trophies just beyond the chain-link fence—they were in a moving truck guarded by two large and muscular black gentlemen—Eye of the Tiger began stalking his prey in the Harlem night.

This was the first Rucker Championship meeting of the twenty-first century, and Bevon Robin, aka "Eye of the Tiger," was showing the New York crowd an electrifying side of his game they had not often seen whenever he was running the backcourt for the Fordham Rams.

That night Robin was indeed boy wonder, taking his place among Rucker immortals with a scintillating 32-point performance to lead Dunk.Net Posse to a 75–60 victory over a Vacant Lot crew led by Charles "I Am My Brother's Keeper" Jones and his brother Lamont.

"This is a great feeling, especially the way things have gone for me at Fordham the past three years," said Robin, who was named the championship game's most valuable player. "I've never had a winning season at Fordham, but winning a Rucker Championship helps to ease some of that pain."

That entire 2000 season, Eye of the Tiger had ranked among the league's scoring leaders. By playoff time his 23 points per

game placed him fourth behind Kareem Reid, Ray Rivera of
LIU, and Jamaal "Mel Mel The Abuser" Tinsley, the Indiana
Pacers guard who would take the NBA by storm his rookie
season.

Teaming with a player named "High Five," otherwise known
as Reggie Freeman, the former University of Texas star who took
his perimeter game to Turkey, and "Leave Him Alone Jerome,"
aka Jerome Allen, the former Penn star who ran for a while with
the Minnesota Timberwolves, Eye of the Tiger rose to the challenge of his backcourt rivals as the Joneses simply could not
keep up with the Posse's blink-of-an-eye transition game and
overall athleticism.

For the Posse, who began a new century the way they had
ended an old one, it was a second straight EBC Championship
in Rucker Park. The back-to-back feat had last been pulled off
by the Pyramid All-Stars in the summer of 1986.

Eye of the Tiger's MVP campaign began with a three-pointer
from the parking lot that gave the Posse an early 5–0 lead. From
there, the Tiger's mighty roar filled the caged park.

With 11 minutes, 30 seconds to play in the first half, the six
two sweet-shooting guard with the mighty springs in his muscular legs soared from the foul line, Jackie Jackson–like, attempting a monstrous two-handed jam that would have traveled south
through the cords had he not been pushed from behind by
"Whole Lotta Game," Adrian Walton.

With the crowd in a terrible tizzy and apartment lights from
the Polo Grounds projects flicking on at the kind of alarming
rate that made the dark buildings light up like huge, brick
switchboards, the Tiger pounced again. Late in the first half he
took a pass from a tall, lean teammate named "African Slinky,"

then drained his fourth three-pointer of the evening to give the Posse a 27–20 lead.

"At that point, I knew Bevon wasn't going to let us lose," said High Five Freeman, who added 13 points in the historic battle. "The guy was unconscious out there."

With 10:45 left in the game, the Tiger took another pass, this one from a Latino teammate nicknamed "Carlito's Way" on the right baseline, cradled the ball as he went north and over the outstretched fingertips of two defenders, and shook rust off the rim with a volcanic windmill jam that gave the Posse a commanding 47–35 lead and brought the Rucker faithful onto the court to celebrate.

"I've worked real hard all summer long on my game and it really paid off tonight," the Tiger said after that game from way atop the shoulders of several teammates. "So many great players have come through this park over the years and made their mark.

"Tonight," the Tiger roared, "it was my turn."

Sunshine Comes Back

Forty years later, Danny "Sunshine" Doyle was back at Rucker Park. Sunshine was not there to taunt the mostly black competition or the mostly black audience, a routine the king of Queens had made famous back in the days when he wore a younger man's sneakers, back in the days when he chose selling soda over playing in the NBA.

On this day, Sunshine was there to root for another white kid trying to make a name for himself in the world-renowned, mostly black theater, where some of the top high school players in New York City were set to square off against some of Philly's finest ballplayers, keeping alive a tradition that stretched back to the days of Wilt Chamberlain and Cal Ramsey, Jay Norman and The Helicopter, Herman Knowings.

"Welcome to Rucker Park," the man behind the microphone shouted, "where dreams are born and legends are made."

Through dark glasses, Sunshine watched his son, Tim, a basketball star at St. Dominic's High School on Long Island, walk onto Holcombe Rucker's stage and create another piece of hoop history. The Doyles would become the first white father-and-son combination to have played in the park.

"It kind of gives me goose bumps to see Tim out there, because I see a lot of myself in him," Sunshine said to me that day. "I'm very proud of the fact that this great tradition has been passed down to my son.

"Hell," said Sunshine, wiping away a tear that escaped from beneath his dark glasses, "where did the time go?"

Tim Doyle, a handsome six six swingman ticketed to play his college ball at St. John's, joined forces on the New York squad with a pair of standouts from All Hallows High School: Marvin "Whole Lotta Scholarships" McCullough, a heady player heading to Iona whose father, Bob McCullough, was instrumental in keeping the Pied Piper's dream alive long after Harlem's mentor had died; and Ricky Soliver, a highly recruited player at the Division I collegiate level who was trying to keep up the grades and avoid making an initial stop at a prep school or junior college.

"I gotta tell you," Baby Sunshine said, "being a white kid from the suburbs, and playing in front of all those black people, I was really kind of nervous out there when the game began."

Which explains why Baby Sunshine's first field goal attempt

sailed high over the rim, the suburban brick nearly shattering the glass before it was put out of its misery by one of Philly's forwards.

"I started hearing it from the crowd," Baby Sunshine said. "They started yelling things like, 'You ain't brought no game, white boy!' "

On the sidelines, Sunshine Doyle shook his head and smiled. "Geez," Sunshine snickered, "I could have done that."

Sitting directly behind me in the huge black crowd, the king of Queens looked around the park and said jokingly, "I wonder if all these people know who I came here to root for today?"

On New York's next possession, Baby Sunshine slowly began winning over the crowd. He went high to snatch a rebound, wheeled, and flung a perfect baseball pass the length of the court of McCullough, who turned it into an easy layup.

On three of New York's next four possessions, Baby Sunshine began turning up the heat index. He drained a triple from the left corner, a deuce from the top of the key, and then went around the world in style, making it look oh-so-threesy from deep along the right sideline.

"I started feeling it," Baby Sunshine said. "Then I heard some people in the crowd start to cheer for me, and my heart started to thump a little bit harder.

"This might sound funny, but as I was running up and down the court, I started thinking of this computer basketball game I have at home," he said. "When you reach the top level of the game, you get to play at Rucker Park. Now here I was, actually playing on this famous court. It was really kind of strange."

Along the sidelines, Sunshine smiled after his boy's three-ball in the side pocket. "That's more like it," he said.

Late in the first half McCullough returned Baby Sunshine's

favor, tossing a long pass just ahead of the field that Doyle caught and dribbled hard toward the basket, two defenders in hot pursuit.

Steaming ahead for a left-handed layup, Baby Sunshine took two long steps and hit the brakes just beneath the basket. As Baby Sunshine ducked, a high-flying Philly defender attempting to swat his shot-attempt flew helplessly out of bounds.

Baby Sunshine elevated, and with the second defender on his back, dropped a soft bank shot into the well.

Then Baby Sunshine got a little carried away. Confident and cocky, he tore a page from his father's old joke book and began doing a helicopter routine as he ran downcourt. As the crowd buzzed, Sunshine Doyle began looking for that old getaway bus that used to hustle him back to Astoria. Meanwhile, one of the officials working the game ran over to Baby Sunshine.

"Do you know what the color of your skin is?" the official asked him. "C'mon, you know the situation out here. I think you'd better watch yourself."

"He was serious," Baby Sunshine said. "I guess he was just looking out for me."

The game seesawed throughout the first half. One Philly fanatic who was not too thrilled with the zebras was shown the door. "Same old garbage," the Philly fanatic said on his way out of Holcombe Rucker's place, "damned New York gettin' all the calls."

Early in the second half New York built a double-digit lead. Baby Sunshine was summoned to the bench for a breather. When Philly cut the deficit to four points, many in the large audience began yelling, "Put Tim in! Put Tim in!"

"I couldn't believe it," Baby Sunshine said. "I guess I was winning them over."

Late in a tied game, Baby Sunshine took an inbounds pass just beneath the New York basket and packed his bags for a coast-to-coast flight. He lost his man with a left-to-right, behind-his-back dribble in the backcourt that got a collective "oohh" from the crowd, zipped past half-court, then split two defenders on his way to the hoop. He put up a lefty-layup, got fouled, and hit a free throw to give New York a 77–74 lead.

After a long, long Philly hold that resulted in a backdoor bucket that trimmed the deficit to 77–76, there still remained 38 seconds.

After a critical New York turnover, Philly took possession and jumped ahead, 78–77, with just three seconds left.

New York worked the ball around to Baby Sunshine for a desperation heave just beyond the half-court stripe. The crowd held its collective breath as ball sailed toward net, but Baby Sunshine's offering clanged high off the back of the rim and over the backboard, giving Philly its bragging rights until the summer of 2002.

"It felt good when it left my hands," Baby Sunshine said. "Man, if I had only hit that shot. . . ."

Despite the final miss, Baby Sunshine led all scorers with 30 points. "I was a little nervous after the game," Baby Sunshine said. "I didn't know what to expect."

Most of the same people who had been booing him earlier in the game left their seats—to congratulate Baby Sunshine. They thanked him for putting on a show and wished him well in Big East battle. Word of Baby Sunshine's magical afternoon spread fast and far, reaching as far as Spain, where St. John's coach Mike Jarvis was piloting a U.S. amateur collegiate team.

"If I live to be a thousand years old," Baby Sunshine said, "I'll never forget that day."

It ended with the Sunshine Boys walking out of Rucker Park not in the company of security guards, but in the company of Baby Sunshine's eight-foot MVP trophy.

"What can I say?" said the king of Queens, his proud smile stretching across the asphalt. "The kid must get it from his father."

Rucker Park Goes Corporate

Greg Marius had seen the bad times, which included the cancelation of his Entertainers Basketball Classic one dark summer in the early 1980s. But as a new century was taking shape, Marius's vision had taken off like one of those Vince Carter flights to the rim. The EBC was finally catching the fancy of corporate America, and sponsors like AT&T and various soft drink companies began pouring the kind of sponsorship money into his pockets that Holcombe Rucker could only have dreamed about.

Marius thanked the Rucker faithful for sticking with him through the good times and bad, penning an open letter to them in the summer of 2001 that was published in a program called "EBC at Rucker Park." Marius began with the following: "It's been a hard nineteen years, but it's been worth it. Way back in 1982, the Entertainers Basketball Classic was born when myself and the rest of the Disco Four (Cool G., Ronnie Dee, Al Cash and Country) challenged the Crash Crew to a game.

"A few years later, I had already given up on the tournament. Our music was slow and the summer seemed slower. But a few strangers walked up to me and asked why I didn't keep up the tournament. They all said they enjoyed it and missed it. Ever since then, I have promised myself that as long as I'm alive, I'll make sure the EBC is too. If and when I retire, I'll pass it to the right people. They'll carry on this tradition that you, the fans, helped build for the world to see."

By the following year, Holcombe Rucker's baby was all grown up, and Marius was its proud and profit-turning papa. For the second straight summer, the games were now being televised at least once a week on cable and satellite television.

Where the Pied Piper had started with two baskets, a few neighborhood players, and a referee's whistle, there were now celebrities, television crews, busloads of tourists, and a steady stream of NBA stars with multimillion-dollar contracts.

Where the Pied Piper's old chalk scoreboard once hung, there were now huge advertising banners for all those corporate sponsors, and a deejay spinning hip-hop during time-outs.

With so many new NBA talents parachuting into the park at a moment's notice, admission lines began forming a half day before game time, and there were now game programs for fans who were reminded that a whole line of merchandise was available at the EBC's league store nearby.

Indeed, this profitable offshoot of Holcombe Rucker's creation now had a website and a corporate marketing division and its own line of merchandise, from clothing to videos of memorable games.

I asked the great Dr. J. what he thought of the Rucker Tournament's flaky new cousin. "The league's not dead; it's just different than what it once was," he said. "But then again, so is the world we live in."

Though NBA stars were not frequenting Rucker Park the way pros did during Dr. J.'s era, current stars like Allen Iverson, Vince Carter, Stephon Marbury, Ron Artest, and Jermaine O'Neal were coming to games, and celebs from Bill Clinton to Mike Tyson could be found sitting in the stands.

College coaches and scouts were also back to take in the ac-

Stephon Marbury, President Bill Clinton, and David Stern at the Rucker *(Rodney Williams)*

tion, hoping to find the next Harthorne Wingo or Joe Hammond, but mostly to watch their own players compete in the summertime classic.

"To me, there is such a pool of untapped talent playing up at the Rucker," said Mike Jarvis, the St. John's coach. "It's the kind of tournament that I encourage my own kids to play in because it can really toughen them up.

"I really enjoy myself when I go up there," Jarvis added. "It's amazing when you think of all the great players that have passed through that park the past fifty-plus years, and so many of them were not just great players, but great people, too."

And, of course, there were the rappers, hip-hop moguls like Sean "P. Diddy" Combs, Fat Joe, and Ja Rule, all of whom were spending thousands of dollars each summer to compete against one another by luring their NBA and streetball pals to The World's Most Famous Playground.

In the meantime, Marius was negotiating merchandising deals with Reebok and the NBA, and other players, at least according to the commish, were using Rucker's grand old stage as a storefront window from which to sell their wares.

Such was the case, Marius said, when Kobe Bryant made a historic visit to Rucker Park in July 2002, just weeks after helping the Los Angeles Lakers capture their third straight championship.

That night Bryant was alternately cheered and heckled while playing in a game with three other NBA players, and had his hands full against a Washington, D.C.–based team led by the playground phenom Prime Objective.

Bryant seemed shaky and scored 14 points and had a missed dunk before a rainstorm canceled the second half. After the game, he admitted being slightly intimidated by the legendary Rucker reputation.

During his appearance, Bryant hugged Hammond, who'd played with Bryant's father, Joe "Jellybean" Bryant, in the old Eastern League.

"Kobe said, 'I've heard so much about you. Rub some of that magic off on me,' " Hammond recalled.

And yet, Marius said, it was not just Rucker magic that brought Bryant to the fabled park, but a shrewd sense of capitalism. After all, Marius said, business is as much a part of today's game as a crossover dribble or slam-dunk.

"Kobe's a clean-cut guy, but he knew that if he wanted to sell

**Greg Marius, the driving force behind the Entertainers Basketball
Classic, with Kobe Bryant and Marius's assistant, Kevin Jones**
(Rodney Williams)

more of his basketball shoes, he needed to make an appearance
in the streets," Marius said.

"Before Kobe visited Rucker Park, the streets were not buying
his shoes," he added.

"He knows that it's the kids who go to the parks who buy
those shoes. So from a corporate standpoint, Kobe made the
right decision."

While Marius would not disclose the actual worth of his
league, he went so far as to tell me and Corey Kilgannon, for an
article we cowrote in the *New York Times* on August 2, 2002,
that his creation had enormous profit potential.

"The league is priceless," he said. "I'm not going to tell you that this is a multimillion-dollar business, not yet, anyway," he said. "But we're about to take off in that direction."

But just before takeoff, not everyone at Rucker Park was as happy as Marius with the direction in which the greatest show on asphalt was headed.

In fact, players like Joe Hammond and other Rucker loyalists began grumbling that the park was being wrung dry as a commercial vehicle, and that commercialization had crept into the game itself, a fact that Marius himself could not deny.

Holcombe Rucker, they said, wouldn't even recognize the place.

"It ain't what Rucker built it to be," Hammond said. "It's a tourist attraction now, a moneymaker, and the big business is killing the basketball."

According to Hammond, Rucker rivalries were now developing not between people with different colored uniforms, but between those with different sponsors.

"I'm the greatest player in the history of this league," Hammond said. "And do you know why you never see me on these Rucker telecasts? That's because Reebok is a major sponsor of the EBC, and I've done some advertising work with Nike, so I guess the thinking there is, 'Screw him, he ain't one of us, he's one of them, so don't put no camera on him.'"

"It's a freak show," Hammond added. "People come up here to laugh now, not watch basketball. It's more like a hip-hop show. These guys wiggle, they wobble, but they can't hit the backboard with a rock. Even when the pros come up, they jump into the same comedy act. No one wants to win, and it ain't getting the players nowhere."

Other devotees lament that the current state of the league has put Harlem's hallowed ground on the auction block for tourists to gawk at, in the manner of Uptown jazz clubs, soul food spots, and churches. With large franchises coming to Harlem, some were calling it Rucker meets Starbucks.

But Marius defended his enterprise, insisting above all things that the level of play at Rucker Park has never been better.

"We're a very, very competitive league," he said. "There isn't a league in New York City or anywhere in the country filled with the kind of talent we have here, and I'm not going to apologize for turning a streetball game into one of the largest marketing tools in corporate America."

So to those who say that the league's founding father wouldn't recognize the place, well, Marius says, why should he? After all, Mr. Rucker doesn't live here anymore.

"The people who say that we aren't a part of the Holcombe Rucker philosophy are right," he said. "But who can deny the fact that my league has kept the legacy of Holcombe Rucker alive?"

Fat Joe and the Terror Squad

In the summer of 2002, Fat Joe's Terror Squad and Artie Green's Ruff Ryders squared off for the EBC Championship.

To that point, the biggest highlight of the playoffs had come to Rucker Park in the smallest of packages. Her name was Shannon Bobbitt, aka "Something Special," a five-foot-two-inch, sixteen-year-old point goddess who had wowed the crowds all season with a handle lethal enough to turn heads in the men's division.

Shannon "Something Special" Bobbitt *(Rodney Williams)*

Running the show for the Lady Mustangs in the women's championship final, Something Special turned garbage time into the time of her young life. With the game against Milbank well in hand in the closing minutes, Something Special put on a dribbling display that would have made Allen Iverson blush, crossing over opponents with a shoelace-poppin' shuffle that had a capacity crowd roaring on its feet.

At one point Something Special avoided defenders closing in

on each side of her by picking up her dribble—without the use of either hand. As the two defenders lunged to her right and left, Something Special dribbled once behind her back, then, using only her right leg, pinned the ball to the seat of her pants, freezing the two defenders in their tracks. That one move sent thousands of park rats scurrying through the aisles in stunned disbelief, high-fiving each other in celebration.

"She's Something Special, Something Special," Duke "Tango" Mills barked as the exhibition wound down. "She's got the meanest first step I've ever seen in my life—put another hundred seconds on the clock for her!"

Moments later Something Special needed help carrying a pair of eight-foot statues out of the park, as she took home her individual championship trophy and the most valuable player award for a season in which she averaged 25 points, 6 assists, and 4 steals per game. Not bad for a young lady who had never played at Rucker Park before that season.

"My basketball talents are a God-given gift," she said after the game. "When I use that gift and get the crowd on my side like I did tonight, that hypes me up."

Something Special, who had just transferred from St. Raymond's, a Catholic hoop power in the Bronx, to Murray Bergtraum, a public school power in Manhattan, already had a few dozen letters from Division I colleges interested in her basketball services.

"I don't know where I'm going," Something Special said as she stepped off the blacktop. "But hopefully I'm on my way."

By the time the men's championship had rolled around, Fat Joe and Mousey had two NBA stars playing for their Terror Squad: Stephon Marbury, The Handler himself, who was now with the Phoenix Suns; and Ron Artest, The True Warrior, now with the Indiana Pacers. Also suiting up for the Terror Squad was former Chicago Bull Charles Jones and his brother Lamont; Stephon's kid brother, Zach "Starbury" Marbury; "The Franchise," John Strickland; Adrian "Whole-Lotta-Game" Walton; and "Best-Kept-Secret" Kareem Reid.

The Ruff Ryders, considerable underdogs entering the contest, were led by Seton Hall's stellar point guard Andre Barrett, aka The One, who opened the contest with a long jumper from the top of the key to put Fat Joe and company in an early 3–0 hole.

As NBA cameras rolled, both teams staged a seesaw clash littered with highlights, including The Franchise's punishing dunk over the Ruff Ryders' talented big man, known only as The Chrysler Building, which gave Terror Squad a 10–7 lead.

Later in the first half, Terror Squad opened up a six-point lead, 32–26, when Zach Starbury and the True Warrior steamed upcourt on a two-on-one fast break that ended with True Warrior slamming home a deuce, then celebrating the flush by floating above the action and slapping the backboard with delight.

Early in the second half, Stephon Marbury executed the most dynamic play of his career, asphalt or hardwood, leaping high above a crowd along the left baseline to grab an alley-oop pass from Best-Kept-Secret, and, still in flight, reverse-jamming over The Chrysler Building. A stunned hush fell over a crowd that had seen a myriad of marvelous Marbury moves throughout the years, but not one like that.

And it was Marbury who buried the biggest bucket of the ballgame, a three-pointer from the top of the key with 7 minutes, 28 seconds remaining to give Terror Squad a 64–63 lead. Fat Joe's crew would not trail thereafter, pulling away for an 80–69 victory and their first-ever Rucker Championship.

"I've been waiting for this all my life," said Fat Joe, a huge diamond nameplate bouncing proudly off his chest and glowing
beneath the bright lights. "It means the world to us," he said.
"We've been at this for five years, and now we finally own the
streets.

"Tonight," Fat Joe said, "I wouldn't want to be anywhere else
in the world."

*When the NBA celebrated its fiftieth anniversary back in 1996,
the league voted on what it considered its fifty greatest players of
all time. Nine of those fifty players were Rucker Park alums:
Abdul-Jabbar, Archibald, Chamberlain, Cowens, Cunningham,
Erving, Frazier, Monroe, and Reed.*

*Somewhere up in basketball heaven, Holcombe Rucker is
smiling.*

EPILOGUE

reg Marius was right. Kobe Bryant did indeed have an ul-
terior motive when he showed up at Rucker Park in July
2002. While Kobe's appearance did a lot to enhance the
Rucker tourney's reputation as the place where even the biggest
stars come for a quality run, the fact remains that Bryant and
other NBA superstars who now play at the park are getting a lot
more out of their asphalt experience than they are giving.

When Rucker Park was rocking in the early 1970s, Kobe's 14-
point performance, which included a missed dunk, would have
been considered a major disappointment from a player of such
magnitude. And though some boo birds were flying around
Kobe's game on that rainy day in Harlem, the only thing that the
Laker great was hearing was the cha-chinging sounds of cash
registers throughout New York City and the rest of the country
taking in money on the sales of the many products he endorses.
Bryant knew full well that no matter how poorly he played that
day, all he really had to do was slip on a tank top, give and take
a few elbows, smile for the ESPN and satellite cameras, and
watch sales of his sneakers and other merchandise soar into another stratosphere.

What better venue for Bryant to market his wares than in
Harlem, New York City, otherwise known as the basketball cap-

ital of the universe? In Harlem, brand-new, expensive sneakers are as much a status symbol as brand-new, expensive automobiles are in places like Hollywood, California, and the rich, mostly white suburbs that surround New York City.

In a nutshell, Kobe's game was a lot slicker than the one he showed on the court that day. His savvy marketing skills not only bolstered his bank account, but also enhanced his basketball legend, as he now stands alongside players like Wilt Chamberlain, Julius Erving, and Connie Hawkins as being among Rucker Park's most famous alumni. On the surface at least, the ultimate basketball warrior made the trek to the ultimate basketball playground, respecting tradition and the talents of the players who make Rucker Park the world's most famous outdoor arena. But the box score from that game will never reveal how many youngsters begged their parents, or busted their piggy banks, for a pair of Kobe hi-tops.

Image. It's everything where sales are concerned. And as the Rucker Tournament grows in popularity with each passing summer, so too will the number of marketing and advertising geniuses who are more concerned with their high-profile clients making profits than making spectacular dunks.

As a result, the overall quality of play in the tiny park will likely suffer, as players like Bryant, Vince Carter, and Allen Iverson rarely return to the Rucker surface after making their much-heralded debuts. This of course is not the case for every NBA star, especially New York playground products like Stephon Marbury and Ron Artest, but even players that connected to the city game are surely thinking dollars and cents every time they step onto Holcombe Rucker's hallowed ground.

With such a revolving door of NBA talent coming in and out

of the park, great rivalries such as the ones that existed between Wilt Chamberlain, Cal Ramsey, and Jackie Jackson back in the 1950s and 1960s have become almost nonexistent.

Even with an increasing number of NBA stars coming to the games, the Entertainers Basketball Classic will never be the competitive wonder that the Rucker League was in its prime, when pro players tested their mettle against other pros as well as battle-tested playground stars.

On the flip side, everyone is now making money. Greg Marius's enterprise is worth a small fortune, as corporations like AT&T and other sponsors have bought into the business of basketball as being more entertainment than sport. When the NBA itself jumps on your bandwagon, you know you've got a good thing going.

In addition, team owners like P. Diddy and Fat Joe get nothing but free publicity from their appearances at the park, and the neighborhood folk who feel a strong connection to such stars whom they feel "made it" but are now "giving back," go out and buy the records and clothes those same stars are hawking as well. Heck, even the top players are getting paid to perform, sometimes several thousand dollars per game, by rappers who want to win, literally, at any cost.

And while admission to Rucker Park remains free, is sitting in the park and being surrounded by corporate banners and getting AT&T T-shirts thrown into your lap really any different now than sitting home and watching all of those commercials on so-called "free TV"?

So when a legitimate playground legend like Joe Hammond tells me that "the league is selling out now to corporate sponsors," what he is really saying is that the league has been stripped of a certain purity that fueled it back in the glory days. When Nate "Tiny" Archibald came to Rucker Park with basketball in hand, he was there to do battle with archrival Pee Wee Kirkland, and not to do a thirty-second sound bite for television in the hope that some young kid at home would go out and purchase something with his name on it.

In fairness to life in Rucker Park as it exists today, past players wanting to get paid have put out their hands as well, but there was no sponsorship money or wealthy entertainer there to grease their palms.

But therein lies the difference between basketball then and now. The great Dr. J., who once asked about being paid, understood the need to play on for the sake of competition and pride, and for the betterment of his overall game.

Most current NBA stars who have guaranteed multimillion-dollar contracts might not be that hungry. Why prove yourself on asphalt when you've already proven yourself on Madison Avenue?

At the end of the day, even if NBA stars are driven to Rucker Park games for their own personal gain, Greg Marius and the rest of the people running the Entertainers Basketball Classic will always welcome them with open arms. Players like Kobe Bryant and Vince Carter and Baron Davis and Shawn Marion not only bring out droves of fans and a number of television cameras, but their collective presence brings to the park a number of quality collegiate and ex-collegiate players that form the bulk of the league's talent core.

In the years ahead, EBC players will be rising into nothing but bright blue skies as the league appears to have only begun to tap into its great profit potential. There has been talk of traveling all-star teams competing against college and pro caliber competition, and an expansion that might include foreign teams that spend their summers touring and competing throughout the United States.

With the games nationally televised, additional sponsors and major advertisers will surely jump on the Rucker bandwagon. Despite its shortcomings, the EBC will continue to thrive off the tradition of basketball excellence established in the park from the 1950s through the early 1980s. The park is rich with memories that other playground venues around the country simply cannot match, and tales, some taller than others, will continue to unfold on that hallowed, windswept patch of blacktop for generations to come.

A NOTE
ABOUT THE AUTHOR

Vincent M. Mallozzi is a native of Harlem who has become the Rucker Tournament's unofficial historian, covering it for such publications as the *New York Times*, the *Village Voice*, the *Source*, *Vibe*, and *Slam*. He was recently elected to the Rucker Hall of Fame for his community service.

An editor in the sports department of the *Times*, he has also been a contributing writer there since graduating from St. John's University and the Technical University of Budapest in Hungary in 1986. An author of two other books on basketball, and a professor of journalism at St. John's, Vincent resides in Aberdeen, New Jersey, with his wife, Cathy, and their two sons, Christopher and Michael.

Printed in the United States
by Baker & Taylor Publisher Services